GODF[REY]
A M

The Valor Of Vision

Practical, Spiritual, and Strategic Guidance for a Vision Driven Life

Trilogy Christian Publishers

A Wholly Owned Subsidiary of Trinity Broadcasting Network

2442 Michelle Drive

Tustin, CA 92780

Copyright © 2024 by Godfred Dodzie Amuzu

Scripture quotations marked AMP are taken from the Amplified® Bible (AMP), Copyright © 2015 by The Lockman Foundation. Used by permission. www.Lockman.org.

Scripture quotations marked (KJV) taken from The Holy Bible, King James Version. Cambridge Edition: 1769.

Scripture quotations marked NKJV are taken from the New King James Version®. Copyright © 1982 by Thomas Nelson. Used by permission. All rights reserved.

All rights reserved, including the right to reproduce this book or portions thereof in any form whatsoever.

For information, address Trilogy Christian Publishing

Rights Department, 2442 Michelle Drive, Tustin, CA 92780.

Trilogy Christian Publishing/ TBN and colophon are trademarks of Trinity Broadcasting Network.

For information about special discounts for bulk purchases, please contact Trilogy Christian Publishing.

Trilogy Disclaimer: The views and content expressed in this book are those of the author and may not necessarily reflect the views and doctrine of Trilogy Christian Publishing or the Trinity Broadcasting Network.

10 9 8 7 6 5 4 3 2 1

Library of Congress Cataloging-in-Publication Data is available.

ISBN 979-8-89333-428-9

ISBN (ebook) 979-8-89333-429-6

DEDICATION

To the Lord my God, who echoed the following words of prophecy in my heart: "Write the vision And make *it* plain on tablets, That he may run who reads it." (Habakkuk 2:2 NKJV)

And to my parents, Joseph and Josephine Amuzu, for planting a sense of vision in me.

ENDORSEMENTS

This book contains a comprehensive composition of the subject matter of Vision. The author has skillfully tackled the topic from multiple dimensions, providing an in-depth and practical application of the knowledge for daily usage. I highly recommend this book to everyone irrespective of your background, profession, religion, or social orientation.

Apostle Samuel Gyau Obuobi
General Secretary: The Church of Pentecost

I am thrilled by the clarity of visibility provided by Prophet Godfred Dodzie Amuzu into the topic of vision. The book provides a gateway to vividly visualize your vision as you journey through the carefully knitted stories, biblical references, and insightful examples enclosed in its pages. The multi-dimensional perspectives of its text generate an engaging and addictive read, with an unceasing desire to explore a deeper understanding of the knowledge area.

I endorse *The Valor of Vision!*

Apostle Emmanuel Agyemang Bekoe
International Missions Director: The Church of Pentecost

As a business owner and leader, I am constantly faced with the opportunity of creating and driving an inspiring vision to promote growth, advance positivity and maintain profitability of my business. Engaging with the teachings of Prophet Godfred Dodzie Amuzu over the years has provided me with the right frame of mind for sound decision-making, a relentless source of inspiration to contend with challenging business environment, and the right leadership skills for creating optimal performance within my workforce. Indeed, I have personally employed the knowledge and principles in this book at my organization and can attest to its efficacy. Therefore, I greatly recommend *The Valor of Vision* for both individuals and institutions who seek advancement in their areas of endeavor.

Ernest Ossei-Boateng
C.E.O: Intercontinental Wealth Network, USA

This book, written by PROPHET GODFRED DODZIE AMUZU, is a tool prepared to remind you of the need for a vision-driven life, how to conceive vision, set achievable goals, and achieve these goals. The author has been a man of vision as far back as I have known him, over 25 years, and has indeed achieved multiple dimensions of great visions in his life. His wealth of experience in achieving his own visions and guiding others over the years in different fields has equipped him with the right knowledge to speak on this topic.

I highly recommend this book to anyone serious about life and wanting to lead a visionary life for themselves or any organization they are leading. Unlike other books that may be read once, this book should be kept close at hand as a reference pool of knowledge at any point in time.

Rev. Fr Ezekiel Farouk SULEY
Catholic Diocese of Navrongo/Bolgatanga- Ghana

I have known and worked closely with Prophet Godfred Dodzie Amuzu since 2018. He is admirably endowed with a remarkable ability to conceive both personal and organizational vision, appropriately cast such vision with colleagues, and subsequently drive it to realization. His vision conception transcends multiple realms, embraces different dimensions of life, and renders him able to brilliantly unveil practical life lessons from inspiring biblical and real life stories. Anchored by many years of experience in vision pursuit, his teachings on the topic are practically transformative, engaging, thought provoking, and a great contribution to the global marketplace of knowledge.

I endorse this book for the development and achievement of both an individual and corporate vision-driven life.

Apostle Michael Agyemang-Amoako
National Head: The Church of Pentecost USA Inc.

The Valor of Vision contains profound and practical teachings on vision, providing deep and detailed dimensions of understanding. In an overwhelmingly fast-paced world, with multiple and competing options in any sphere of life, it takes only the visionaries to identify, pursue and arrive at their destinations. This book provides guidance for accomplishing exactly that.

Philip Gborku
C.E.O Shorthills Investment LLC, USA

Every vision has its appointed time, place and purpose. Prophet Godfred Dodzie Amuzu, in this monograph The *Valor of Vision,* has demystified the intricate notion of vision and its appeal and power to dictate, direct, and divide human lives and destinies. Using his own story and those of others, within the seventeen chapters of his book he has unveiled the whys and hows of vision through the lenses of the Bible and human industry.

I highly recommend this book to anyone who desires to set his or her life on course, as Jesus Christ wants us to. In addition, it is for those who feel inadequate in themselves and afraid of tomorrow to be courageous while relentlessly pursuing their God-given vision.

Apostle Andrews Donkor
President: Pentecost Biblical Seminary, Wayne, New Jersey, USA

ACKNOWLEDGEMENTS

The vision of authoring this book has been made possible through the instrumentality and sacrifice of my dear wife Mrs. Angela E. Amuzu, and my wonderful children: Joshua, Joseph, and Esther. Their relentless encouragement and support fueled this vision into a reality. I am eternally grateful to Apostle Michael and Mrs. Sheila Agyemang Amoako, the national head of The Church of Pentecost U.S.A Inc. for discovering, nurturing, and growing my potential.

The following spiritual parents whom I served under have contributed tremendously towards my spiritual growth. They are Apostle Andrews & Mrs. Evelyn Donkor, Apostle Samuel & Mrs. Mary Arthur, Apostle Augustus & Mrs. Margaret Asemnor, Apostle Dr. John & Mrs. Margaret Appiah, Apostle Stephen & Mrs. Juliet Amponsah, Apostle Seth & Mrs. Esther Asante, and Pastor Saka & Mrs. Agnes Ntiamoah.

I am overwhelmingly grateful to the following vision partners who believed, encouraged, and supported me in diverse ways. They are Mr. Earnest & Deaconess Nana Yaa Ossei Boateng, Elder Robert & Mrs. Margaret Nyarko, and Elder Philip & Mrs. Patience Gborku.

Finally, my heart of gratitude goes to Dr. Ruth Antwi and Mrs. Evelyn Ohene for editing and formatting the manuscript. May the Lord bless you!

TABLE OF CONTENTS

PART ONE (THE FRAMEWORK OF VISION)

CHAPTER ONE: UNDERSTANDING VISION 23

CHAPTER TWO: TYPES OF VISION 33

CHAPTER THREE: SOULISH VISION 39

CHAPTER FOUR: SPIRITUAL VISION 49

CHAPTER FIVE: THE NATURE AND CHARACTERISTICS OF VISION (PART 1) 55

CHAPTER SIX: THE NATURE AND CHARACTERISTICS OF VISION (PART II) 67

CHAPTER SEVEN: PHASES OF VISION 79

CHAPTER EIGHT: THE CONSEQUENCES OF LACK OF VISION 99

CHAPTER NINE: FORMS OF VISION 115

CHAPTER TEN: VISION CASTING AND MAPPING 123

PART TWO (BIBLICAL/SPIRITUAL VISIONS)

CHAPTER ELEVEN: INTRODUCTION TO BIBLICAL/SPIRITUAL VISIONS 131

CHAPTER TWELVE: THE VISION OF GREATNESS (THE ABRAHAMIC VISION) 135

CHAPTER THIRTEEN: THE VISION OF SUCCESS (NEHEMIAH'S VISION) 161

CHAPTER FOURTEEN: THE VISION OF LEADERSHIP 207

CHAPTER FIFTEEN: THE VISION OF ADMINISTRATION - JOSEPH'S VISION 239

CHAPTER SIXTEEN: VISION OF DOMINANCE (JESUS' VISION) 259

CHAPTER SEVENTEEN: VISION CONCLUSION 273

SELECTED BIBLIOGRAPHY 277

ABOUT THE AUTHOR 281

INTRODUCTION

("Vision, then, like love and wisdom, is not something to be lost but the constant gift of God to be fully used." - Unknown)

> *"And the Lord said to Abram, after Lot had separated from him: 'Lift your eyes now and look from the place where you are—northward, southward, eastward, and westward; for all the land which you see I give to you and your descendants forever.'"*
> **Genesis 13:14-15 (NKJV)**

VISION BACKGROUND

My formative years were spent mostly in a small town (Obomeng) in the Kwahu Mountains in West Africa, Ghana. In this town (and mostly the entire Kwahu Area) lies a tale of two worlds: the extremely rich (who were mostly traders and residents in the capital city of Ghana, Accra, and have built their mansions in Kwahu) and the vulnerable poor (who were mostly local residents). My observations from these two worlds unveiled a dimension of adequacy and scarcity that caused me to ask the questions, why do some have and some don't? My curiosity stemmed from an observation of scarcity and poverty that eclipsed most individuals, families, and communities in these towns. As an introverted child, this sense of curiosity was not evident in an external exploration or in my conversations, but rather an internal contemplation and comparison of the characteristics that marked these two different worlds, life of abundance and life of scarcity. What is the difference between these two worlds that has created such a wide gap in terms of resources accessibility and usage? My question lingered.

Educational: At the onset and throughout my formal education, I have met students who were very intelligent academically, but that intelligence did not translate into a commensurate standard of living. Contrarily to that are those who were not academically brilliant but have carved an appreciable standard of living and accomplished great things in life. Therefore, two individuals may experience the same level of formal education, but their life achievements may be different. What could possibly be the reason? This question lingered!

Professional: In any career or profession, I have observed that you may start two individuals at the same entry-level position in the same organization, providing them with the same level of opportunities, and you are certain they will not be at the same level on the professional ladder or paygrade in the next five to ten years' time. This means that commencing work in the same company on the same day at the same position does not guarantee the same level of achievement with the passage of time. Indeed, what could be the possible differentiating factor? The question still lingered!

Spiritual: Even on the level of spirituality, believers are all granted the same grace of God; however, the level of accomplishment is never the same. There is a visible difference, which may be attributed to many possible different reasons. Although I may not be able to list and treat all the possible reasons here, there is always a fundamental push-pull factor that causes a differentiation in every dimension of human life. In my framework of curiosity, I wondered if I could decipher the possible causes of success as compared to failure.

Corporate: The differentiating factors that cause distinguishing levels of achievement in individual lives also impact organizations, corporate bodies, and nations as well. Natural resource availability, or the absence thereof, does not determine the level of achievements and eventual standard of living attained by members of an institution. Unfortunately, there is enough compelling evidence across the globe that confirms the validity of this statement. There are many countries that abound in natural resources but whose citizens are languishing in poverty and the opposite is also true.

MY DISCOVERY

If all the above scenarios and sentences are true, then it is imperative for a journey of discovery to be undertaken, to ascertain the causative agent of this differentiation. It is against this backdrop that my mental curiosity was translated into an inquisition of understanding, leading to the discovery of the word "VISION." Why vision? What is it? What does it do? How does it apply? To whom does it apply? How does it influence life? The questions were endless.

WHY IS IT IMPORTANT TO TALK ABOUT VISION?

Vision is one of the most visible agents of change, growth, and success and is relevant in every dimension of human life. Its effect applies to an individual as much as an organization. Throughout the journey of life, one can only go as far as your vision will permit. A great, fulfilling lifestyle is born out of vision. Stability in families is visible and achievable through the lens and power of vision. Societal transformation is effected through the agent of vision, runs on the wheels of vision, and sustained through the force of vision.

Vision provides a sense of direction and destination and ensures the fulfillment of purpose. It is the sustaining force of growth, technological advancement, innovation, and a path of progress and civilization. Life without vision is haphazard, aimless, frustrating, and has no impetus for growth, success, and sustenance. The impact of vision transcends the largest institution through the smallest group, the biggest individual to the smallest person and the largest organ to the tiniest cell.

THE GREAT TRAGEDY

With this magnitude of impact, one may wonder why this topic is not taught in schools. Why is it not commonly discussed in homes, at the dinner table, or preached about in churches? Why are corporate executives not prioritizing the deployment of this knowledge to increase productivity or improve upon service delivery? It is ironic but tragic that such wealth of information is hidden in plain sight while many carry their potential and unfulfilled visions to the graveyard. Others have sadly traversed the face of the earth without fulfilling their God- given purpose.

What We Will Learn in This Book.

This book is an instructional manual for everyone, irrespective of your background, religion, gender, age, or social status. It is a practical, spiritual, transformative, and strategic manual with multiple keys to access the path of vision and the door of success. This book was written with you in mind; therefore, the biblically-based practical applications are viable seeds to greatness, success, distinguished leadership with principles to ensure sustenance, and continuity. The information in this book is applicable to individuals as well as corporate bodies or institutions.

INTRODUCTION

More specifically, the first part of this book treats the framework of vision, which will help you:

- Understand the meaning of vision and it influence on individuals as well as corporate bodies.

- Understand the nature and characteristics of vision in order to position you to operate appropriately.

- Appreciate the consequences of visionless life for an individual and an institution.

- Discover the types and forms of vision, how to conceive each type and nurture it to realization.

- Understand the phases of vision, how to properly transition your vision through the phases, the key requirements and benefits of each phase.

- Identify the measures needed to prevent premature birth of visions.

- How to rightfully cast and map your vision to identify an optimal path of implementation and manage potential risk.

The second part of this book focuses on extracting practical developmental lessons from certain biblical stories. Through these lessons, you will:

- Discover "The Vision of Greatness," which teaches the path, principles, and practicality of achieving greatness in life.

- Understand "The Vision of Success,": "The Orbit of Success" revolves around problem, prayer, people, planning, persistence, patience, priority, purpose, potential, and passion and is determined by ability, attitude and effort.

- Encounter "The Vision of Leadership": "The Leadership Stairs" unveils a detailed path to accomplishing distinguishing leadership.

- Unearth "The Vision of Administration": This lesson teaches how to develop administrative skills and presents practical ways of administering an organization. The applicable scope spans from a simple family unit to a global/multinational institution.

- Appreciate "The Vision of Dominance": Here you will learn how to build a sustainable multigenerational organization that runs on values and principles geared towards fostering continuity. Through these lessons, you will discover the secret of the greatest organization in human history, whose global dominance continues to expand amidst fears of opposition and the values that have ensured its sustenance and continuity.

I have strategically provided a vision motivational quotation, scripture, and vision story at the beginning of every chapter to serve as a thought-provoking inspiration for my readers and cater to the needs of readers from diverse background. As you mine through the pages of this book, the wisdom nuggets you excavate will probably fuel a passionate of vision in you, remove any scale that has blocked your vision, or expel any cloud on your vision. You will begin to experience a great sense and desire for accomplishment, which will ignite a strong, relentless passion for vision pursuit. With a unity of purpose, let us embark on this adventure together. Your life will never be the same after these discoveries.

Now let's get started!

INTRODUCTION

HOW TO USE AND BENEFIT FROM THIS BOOK

I encourage readers to first read through the entire book at least once. Subsequently, I urge you to revisit the book with targeted reading, focusing on the chapters and section(s) that are pertinent to your interest and development for a more in-depth and detailed understanding.

I have included diagrams and tables as visual aids to facilitate deeper engagement with the content. In addition, I have included a few exercises that may provide alternative paths to understanding. I highly recommend the development of your vision map irrespective of your area of interest and encourage you to make it visible for your continuous engagement, update, and re-planning. Organizations may follow the steps indicated in the book to develop their vision map as well and make it visible to every member. Any organization that desires an in-depth teaching on any area may also contact my team for the necessary arrangement or visit the various sites for additional teachings.

If you benefit from the content of this book, be sure to share or recommend it for your family members, friends, church members, or professional colleagues. The world is highly endowed with enough natural resources, and we are better off if our family members, teachers, managers, community and church leaders have a better understanding of vision and its application. Let us envisage and tread on a path of vision for the attainment of a better world!

PART ONE (THE FRAMEWORK OF VISION)

CHAPTER ONE

UNDERSTANDING VISION

(VISION CAN SEE THE MOUNTAINTOP EVEN WHEN THE CLOUDS HIDE IT FROM VIEW)

"Then the LORD answered me and said: "Write the vision And make it plain on tablets, That he may run who reads it. For the vision is yet for an appointed time; But in the end, it will speak, and it will not lie. Though it tarries, wait for it; Because it will surely come, It will not tarry."

Habakkuk 2: 2-3 NKJV

"Where there is no vision, the people perish: but he that keepeth the law, happy is he."

Proverbs 29:18 NKJV

VISION STORY-ELON MUSK

Elon Musk was born on June 28, 1971, in Pretoria, South Africa and he has one of the most genius brains in the history of humanity. He is either the CEO, founder, co-founder, owner, or chairman of the following companies: Zip2, X.com (now PayPal),

SpaceX, Tesla Motors, SolarCity (now Tesla Energy), Neuralink, the Boring Company, Twitter/X, the Musk Foundation, OpenAI, and xAI. His revolutionary and transformative vision has impacted everything from space exploration, transportation, energy, and artificial intelligence to financial systems and many more. Musk has a vision that is expressed in this statement about the human species: **"We need to become a multiplanetary species to ensure our survival in the face of potential calamities on Earth."** He hopes to see a self-sufficient city on Mars in the future, while also addressing the urgent need to combat the climate crisis. His vision includes an aircraft that can transport people from New York City to any part of the world within an hour. As far back as history remembers, Homo sapiens has been a uniplanetary species. Musk's vision is setting the pace for further exploration of the possibility of humanity to thrive on other planets.

INTRODUCTION

One of the most powerful transformative forces on earth is the power of vision. It is the ability to see the invisible and make it possible. Vision is the visual manifestation of a person or organization's future. Below are some definitions of the word vision:

- Richard Lynch defines vision as "a challenging and imaginative picture of the future role and objectives of an organization, significantly going beyond its current environment and competitive position." (2006)

"Vision is one of the most powerful transformative forces on earth."

- El-Namaki defines vision as "a mental perception of the kind of environment that an organization aspires to create within a broad time horizon and the underlying conditions for the actualization of this perception." (1992)

- Vision is "an ideal that represents or reflects the shared values to which the organization should aspire." — Kirkpatrick et. Al. (2014)

- Vision is "an ambition about the future, articulated today, it is a process of managing the present from a stretching view of the future." — Dunphy and Stace (1993)

All the above definitions present a diverse perspective of the meaning of vision; however, the commonality is a future state of either an individual or an organization, a state where the elements of growth, success, transformation, engagement, and identity are vivid and viable for the manifestation of an ambition. Therefore, it is related to ambitions, dreams, goals, and objectives but expressed in a futuristic pictorial visualization. The old adage "A picture is worth a thousand words" is true in attempting to define the meaning of vision. Vision is expressed as a picture of the future state.

Many people have visions for various aspects of their lives such as career, education, family, spirituality etc. Some organizations have also vividly expressed their visions, which serve as a North Star for navigating their path to success. Whether for an individual or an organization, a vision must have certain inherent characteristics in order to determine its viability. Below are some characteristics of a good vision.

> *"A vividly expressed vision serves as the north star for navigating your path to success."*

CHARACTERISTICS OF A GOOD VISION

1. CLARITY OF VISION: (HABAKKUK 2.2)

Clarity of vision means that it should be specific and understandable. There must be clarity in a vision; every good vision should be clearly visualized until a vivid image is formed in the mind and can be unambiguously defined. Kazuo Inamori emphasized, "A clear vision produces tremendous confidence, fortifies your will to work hard, motivates others, and leads them to success." (Inamori, 1995) An unclouded vision incites desire for attainment. Vision requires faith because it is normally clear enough to look scary or ignite the fear of impossibility. However, the desire incited by the clarity of the vision and its attainment ignites an inner confidence and assurance for its pursuit. The scripture buttresses the point of clarity by stating that one should "make it plain on tablets…" This means that the vision must be devoid of professional or academic jargon, considering that the vision partners may be people of different professional and academic levels. A well-defined vision is easy to read and understand. As you read this book, take a pause here and write down your vision for your life; make it clear for easy understandability.

UNDERSTANDING VISION

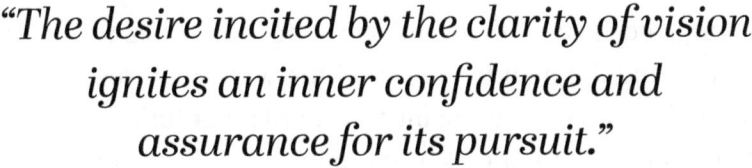

"The desire incited by the clarity of vision ignites an inner confidence and assurance for its pursuit."

2. THE VISION SHOULD BE SOLUTION(S)-BOUND: (NEHEMIAH 1:3; GENESIS 41:28-32)

Every good vision must be solution-bound; that is, the solution must be relevant. The realization of the vision must provide a solution to either an existing problem or a potential problem. Vision should be oriented toward solving a current or future problem(s). Solution is the bridge between the current and future states; therefore, if the solution prevails, the individual/organization is moved closer to its intended future state. On the other hand, if the problem prevails, the individual/organization is brought back to its current state and the gap between the current and future states is widened.

Vision Diagram

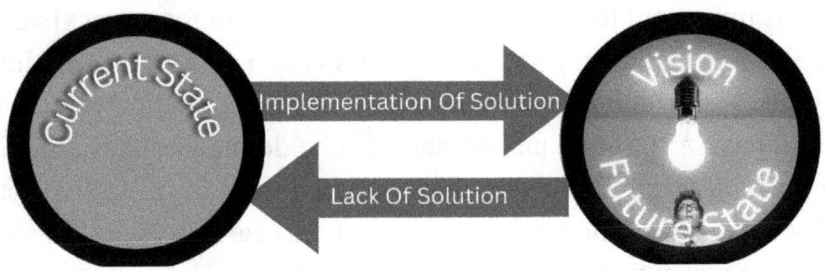

In Nehemiah Chapter 1, we read how Nehemiah understood an existing problem after receiving the news of the precarious state of Jerusalem. He comprehended the current security risk to the inhabitants of Jerusalem due to its broken walls. Nehemiah's act of seeking the face of God and the king, returning to Jerusalem, and mobilizing the people to rebuild the walls of Jerusalem within fifty-two (52) days were meant to provide a solution to the security threat upon the nation (Nehemiah 12). The absence of walls to protect the city meant the people were vulnerable and could be invaded by an enemy without much resistance. Thus, the security threat was an existing problem, his vision was a well-protected state, and the solution was the building of the walls of Jerusalem.

On the other hand, Joseph understood from the dream of Pharaoh that there was a potential future problem to manifest after seven years (Genesis 41:15-31). Joseph understood the meaning of Pharaoh's dream and the possible impending problem (Genesis 41: 28-32). The vision was a future Egypt with minimal or no impact of the then imminent famine on its citizens. The solution was to devise a strategy to combat the potential problem of famine through the gathering, storage, and distribution of food. I will discuss Joseph's vision for Egypt in chapter fifteen.

3. THE VISION SHOULD BE TIME-BOUND: (GENESIS 41:29-30)

It is important to have a well-defined timeline for every vision. The Prophet Habakkuk was told that his vision was for an appointed time. Vision should not be indefinite! Implementation of vision should have a start and an end date and be defined as short, medium, or long-term. The vision that triggered the administrative setup by Joseph was for a total duration of 14 years divided into two halves of seven years each (Genesis 41:29-30). The first strategy, which was implemented during the seven years of abundance, was for collection and storage, and the second strategy was for distribution of the stored food. This vision had a well-defined timeline that left no room for speculation. God's vision for creation was a six-day period and a seventh day for rest (Genesis 1). From the conception through the realization of every vision, it must be measured within a timeframe. Having a well-defined timeline helps to set the pace for transitioning through the phases as well as create an impetus of motivation. For example, since the timeline defines the pace, it helps you to pause and recalibrate your speed during the phases. A vision that is not time-bound may have no sense of urgency and probably slide into an indefinite implementation. Remember, time is a limited resource and must be used wisely. No one has an unlimited supply of time; even if so, sometimes nature will determine the time to implement certain visions. For example, if your vision is athletic-related, then it will be prudent to set its realization before the age of thirty. This is because nature may set limitations after a certain age is attained. Therefore, both individuals and corporate visionary leaders must recognize and provide a timeline for their visions realization.

4. VISION SHOULD BE MEASURABLE

The measurability of a vision is understood by setting up parameters to determine its achievement. Vision is not wishful thinking; therefore, parameters for its realization must be clear, i.e. trackable benchmarks of success. It should be possible to determine when your vision is achieved. The factors that will help you realize the achievement of your vision are the measurable factors.

5. VISION SHOULD BE ACHIEVABLE

The achievability of a vision is such that its elements can be realized within current resources at your disposal or future resource provision. Many visions are conceived amid arid resources, but the ability to see beyond current insufficiency still makes them achievable. Therefore, for a vision to be considered achievable, one must either have enough resources (which is mostly not the case) or strongly believe in divine providence (this is usually the case for most visions).

Chapter Summary

- Vision is one of the most powerful transformative forces on earth.

- Characteristics of good vision are measurable parameters that ensure the quality of a vision.

- Clarity of Vision: Every good vision should have clarity and be well defined.

- Solution-Bound: Every good vision should be solution bound: Implementation of a vision must provide solution to an existing or impending problem.

- Time-Bound: Implementation of every good vision should be time bound. Such time can be categorized as short, medium, or long term. Duration can also be defined by specific times such as years, months, weeks, or days.

- Measurability: Every good vision should have measurable parameters that defines its achievement.

- Achievable: The vision should be achievable, meaning the elements of the vision can be realized within the current resources or future resource provisions.

CHAPTER TWO

TYPES OF VISION

("What would be worse than being born blind?
To have sight without vision." Helen Keller)

In Damascus there was a disciple named Ananias. The Lord called to him in a vision, "Ananias!" "Yes, Lord," he answered. The Lord told him, "Go to the house of Judas on Straight Street and ask for a man from Tarsus named Saul, for he is praying. In a vision he has seen a man named Ananias come and place his hands on him to restore his sight." Acts 9:10-12

VISION STORY-BARACK OBAMA

On January 20th, 2009, the attention of the world was drawn to a 47-year-old African American's inauguration ceremony as the 44th president of the United States of America. Barack Obama had broken through every possible barrier and made history by becoming the first African American to occupy the office of the presidency of the United States. His journey to the apex of American government was fueled by a clear vision that a blessed life should be lived in the service of others and the application of hard work, education, values from the heartland and a middle-class upbringing from a strong family.

Born on August 4, 1961, in Hawaii to Barack Sr., a Kenyan economist, and Stanley Ann Dunham, Barack Obama spent his early childhood in Indonesia after the divorce of his parents and remarriage of his mother to an Indonesian. He returned to Honolulu to live with his maternal grandparents. He received a Columbia University education in political science and international relations and subsequently attended Harvard Law School, where he attracted national attention as the first African American president of the Harvard Law Review. In his memoir *Dreams from My Father* (1995), Obama describes the complexities of discovering his identity in adolescence, the numerous hurdles he overcame and the opportunities he embraced. On his inauguration to the office of the president, Obama was faced with many challenges—an economic collapse, major wars in Iraq and Afghanistan, and the continuing menace of terrorism. His story is one of a vision and inspiration to millions of people around the world.

INTRODUCTION

St. Augustine of Hippo divided vision experiences into three main types. Below is a summary of St. Augustine of Hippo's explanation of the types of vision.

CORPOREAL VISION

Physical sighting. A supernatural manifestation of an object to the eyes of the body. It may take place in two ways: either a figure really present strikes the retina and there determines the physical phenomenon of the vision, or an agent superior to man directly modifies the visual organ and produces in the composite a sensation equivalent to that which an external object would produce. [1]Underhill refers to this vision type as "little else than an uncontrolled externalization of inward memories, thoughts, or

---

1 "Visions and Apparitions". NewAdvent.org. Retrieved 16 July 2018.

intuitions."[2]

IMAGINATIVE VISION

An imaginary vision is defined as one where nothing is seen or heard by the senses of seeing or hearing, but where the same impression is received that would be produced upon the imagination by the senses if some real objects were perceived by them.[3] Niels Christian Hvidt refers to them as visions recognized through mechanisms of the human psyche that are made up of things a soul has acquired through contact with reality.[4]

INTELLECTUAL VISION

The Catholic dictionary defines this as supernatural knowledge in which the mind receives an extraordinary grasp of some revealed truth without the aid of sensible impressions, and mystics describe them as intuitions that leave a deep impression.[5]

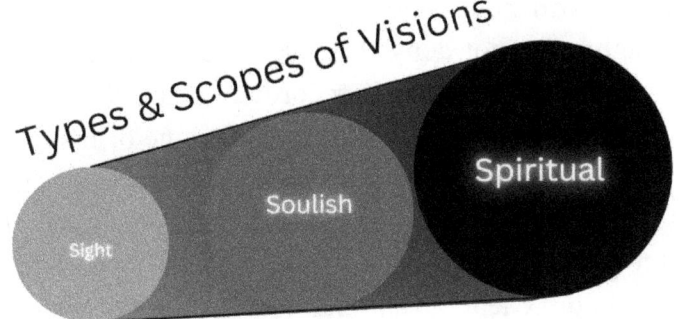

---

[2] "Visions and Apparitions". NewAdvent.org. Retrieved 16 July 2018.

[3] Saint Teresa (of Avila) (1852). The Interior Castle, Or The Mansions. T. Jones. Retrieved 26 July 2018.

[4] Hvidt, N.C. (2007). Christian Prophecy: The Post-Biblical Tradition. Oxford University Press, USA. p. 137. ISBN 978-0-19-531447-2. Retrieved 16 July 2018.

[5] "INTELLECTUAL VISION". catholicculture.org. Retrieved 16 July 2018.

Visions manifest themselves in three distinct types. The type of vision is a description of the source, means, channel or form of its manifestation. St. Augustine's classification of vision focuses on the humanistic type but omits vision from the spiritual realm. Therefore, I have categorized vision into three types according to the nature of its conception, source, and the channel of its manifestation. These are sight, soulish, and spiritual visions. My categorization combines Augustine's imaginative and intellectual together as soulish and introduces a new type of vision called spiritual.

1. PHYSICAL VISION (SIGHT)

Physical vision is sight conceived through the visualization of physical objects. This is natural vision, which is equated to sight. You can see natural things because this type of vision resides in the natural realm. If you can see, then you have this type of vision. Physical vision or sight may be impaired by natural elements such as age or enhanced by objects like magnifying lenses. It is very much treated in the field of medicine and is not the focus of my teaching so I will not spend much time on it. However, the absence of sight may not deny the visionary access to both soulish and spiritual visions. A story is recorded in Acts 9:1-12. Saul was strongly persecuting the church and during one of his expeditions to Damascus, he had an encounter with the Lord Jesus Christ. This encounter resulted in Saul's blindness (loss of sight). However, the Lord told Ananias in a vision (spiritual) that Saul had also had a spiritual vision. Clearly, Saul had lost his natural vision or sight (blindness) but could still have spiritual vision. "And in a vision he has seen a man named Ananias coming in and putting his hand on him, so that he might receive his sight." Acts 9:12. The absence of Saul's physical vision did not deny him access to spiritual vision. These three types of vision are distinct and independent of each other. Therefore, a person with physical vision (sight) may still lack either or both soulish and spiritual vision.

NO	SIGHT AND VISION COMPARISON	
	SIGHT	VISION
1	Those who live by sight live for the moment	Those who live by vision live for both the moment and the future
2	Sight is a function of the eye	Vision is a function of the soul/spirit
3	The framework of sight is natural and limited	The framework of vision is supernatural and unlimited
4	Sight shows current existence	Vision shows what is possible in the future
5	Sight requires no faith	Vision is sustained by faith
6	Non-visionaries walk by sight	Visionaries walk by faith
7	The scope of sight is always smaller than the scope of vision	The scope of vision is always larger than the scope of sight

"The framework of vision is supernatural and unlimited."

Chapter Summary

- St. Augustine of Hippo identified three types of visions, namely: corporeal, imaginative and intellectual.

- I have categorized vision as physical, soulish, and spiritual based on the source, means, channel or form of its manifestation.

- Physical vision is equated to sight; sight is significantly different from vision.

- The table above gives a comparison and contrast between sight and vision.

CHAPTER THREE

SOULISH VISION

("Cherish your visions and your dreams, as they are the children of your soul, the blueprints of your ultimate achievements."
– Napoleon Hill)

> *"During the night, the mystery was revealed to Daniel in a vision. Then Daniel praised the God of heaven."*
>
> **Daniel 2:19**

VISION STORY-BILL GATES

Many years ago, the young Bill Gates conceived a vision that during his lifetime there would be **"universal computing at home and in the office."** This vision was espoused at the time that only big companies could afford a single or a few computers for the entire organization. Microsoft's vision has now grown **"to help people and businesses throughout the world realize their full potential."** This vision statement shows that the company presents its computing products as tools that people and businesses/organizations can use for their personal or organizational development. As of today, the vision of universal computing has been achieved in his lifetime. Not only are there computers in every home and office, there are literally computers in every hand. Nothing is impossible for the visionary!

INTRODUCTION

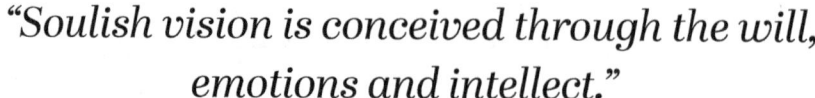

"Soulish vision is conceived through the will, emotions and intellect."

Soulish vision is the type of vision conceived in the soul of an individual. This type of vision can be conceived through will, emotions, and intellect. It resides in the soul, and therefore, even a nonspiritual person has the ability to conceive and birth this kind of vision. This vision fuels many individuals or corporate ambitions. Some of the greatest visions humanity has experienced came out of the souls of people. Some means by which soulish vision can be conceived are; out of necessity, planning, life experiences, self-reflection, or an encounter with knowledge. It is usually the desire to fulfill a need, an encounter with knowledge or reality that ignites the conception of soulish vision. The following triggers of soulish vision may be encountered at various ages and through various means.

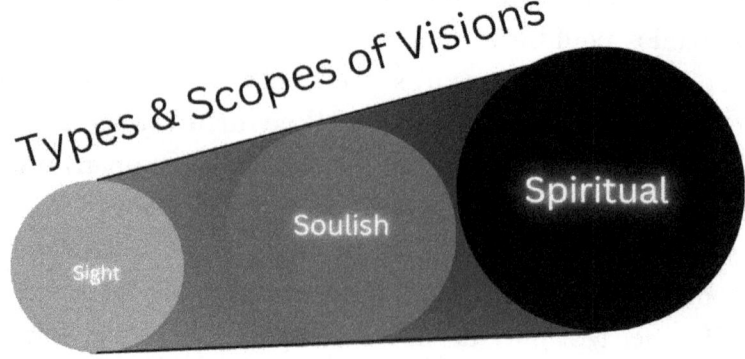

FIVE TRIGGERS OF SOULISH VISION

1. NECESSITY

It is said that necessity is the mother of invention. Some inventions are progressive while others are destructive or retrogressive. People are more likely to conceive soulish vision out of necessity rather than out of abundance. Many visions have been triggered by needs and their implementations have resulted in the alleviation of those needs. Most soulish visions are the result of man's quest or desire to make their world a better place or fulfill a need. Some needs have the potential to compel humanity beyond their comfort zone, resulting in the quest for innovation. Visions conceived and realized out of necessity demonstrate how human beings can achieve almost anything if they are determined and are willing to do so.

2. PLANNING:

Planning may be defined as the process of identifying, prioritizing, and organizing activities or tasks to achieve a desired goal. Proper planning is essential for achieving success in every endeavor of human life. It is often said that invariably, failing to plan is planning to fail. Usually, planning unveils a bigger circumference and a deeper depth of realities and may trigger the conception of vision. Many visions have been conceived, nurtured, and matured through the process of planning. Sometimes the realities, alternatives and possibilities become clear through the process of planning.

The vision to author a book on vision was conceived during one of my regular planning sessions. As I sat down to plan my next area of knowledge development, it became clear to me that

God had given me knowledge in vision and that knowledge may be beneficial and potentially transformative to many lives. With this realization, I started putting my thoughts together, organized a series of teachings on the subject matter to my congregation, and the response was instant and overwhelming. A lady sent me a message, "I wish I knew this 22 years ago." Another person said, "This teaching has the potential to uplift individuals, organizations, communities, and nations from the abyss of failure to the apex of success." Then the Monday after my initial session, a member of the congregation called to encourage me to publish a book on vision with an offer to support. He postponed an important business assignment just to be part of the teaching series on vision to the end. These responses and many more were so encouraging to me that I started organizing my thoughts into components, which later became the chapters of this book. The trigger for this vision was based on a planning session. Planning your life, business, marriage, career, or ministry is essential and may open the door to identifying a vision to pursue.

3. LIFE EXPERIENCES

Experiences define our knowledge, perspective, perception, and reality. Certain experiences such as danger, need, competition, desire for change, disaster, frustration, wars, and many more are triggers of soulish vision. On a higher level, economic, social, political, academic, and technological experiences may trigger vision conception in an individual. In other words, experiences that affect our emotions, will, or intellect are potential triggers of soulish vision.

"There can always be a positive outcome from any negative experience."

Life experiences alone do not determine and define who we become, but our responses to those experiences inform the outcome and influence our lives. Some bad experiences have generated positive outcomes while the opposite is also true. Tough experiences create strong men and easy times create weak men. Therefore, times of adversities must not be seen as an opportunity to quit, but rather an avenue to refine or create your vision. You may be experiencing difficulties in life and contemplating giving up but know that every adversity is a potential trigger of vision. The question is, what lesson have you learned from your adversities? What opportunity do you see from your adversity? One distinguishing feature of visionaries is that they do not allow adversities to define their destiny, nor do they allow such experiences to determine the pursuit of their visions. There can always be a positive outcome from any kind of negative experience. Whether your experience is a loss of job or loved one, stagnation of business or derailment of career, decline of spirituality or academic pursuit, unsuccessful adventure of marriage or ministry, always know that you have the potential to create positive outcome from such perceived negative experiences. Yes, you may not have the ability to control what happens to you, but you can control how you respond to it. Do not brood over negativity, do not cry over spilled milk, do not beat yourself up over your failures. Get up and stand up, shake the dust of failures off, for you are wiser; reset your eyes on the goals and relaunch the vision. Whatever vision your experiences have triggered, hold on to it, gather the relevant knowledge and develop the right skills, look for the provision and go to work, chase it with all your heart and soul, look not to the left or to the right, fix your eyes on the vision and massage it into your life, pursue it like there is no other option, and I can assure you, it is only a matter of time until the vision will become a reality.

4. SELF-REFLECTION

The core position of conceiving vision through self-reflection hinges on the discovery of reality. Time of sober self-reflection and introspection is when an individual gives a serious thought or consideration about their lives, achievements, goals, purpose, failures, and vision. Some people have truly discovered the reality of their lives during these moments of sober self-reflection and deeper introspection. The self-awareness discovered during these times helps to see yourself clearly, objectively, and apprehend your vulnerability. During moments of introspection, the reality of your position against potential, challenges against opportunities, abilities against possibilities and the gap between your current state and future states become clear. Those who take time to productively reflect (not worry) on their lives are in a better position to make decisions that may lead to achieving their visions in life compared to those who engage in barely any self-reflection.

"Moments of sober self reflection are opportunities for reality check."

Many visions have been conceived during times of sober self-reflection. I want to encourage everyone to develop a habit of allocating and observing times of reflection. When you consistently take about fifteen minutes daily to engage in introspection, it helps you to maintain your focus on the important things in life. Moments of self-reflection are times of reality check and may help those who may be drifting away to come back to their planned path of success. These are some of the questions to consider during reflection: Who am I? What is my purpose in life? What have I achieved? What are some of my strengths, weaknesses, and potential? Where do I see myself in the short, medium, and long term? What is the one thing I would love to do consistently even if I am not paid for it? The attempt to answer some of these questions may trigger a vision and potentially set you on the path of success. Do not forget to write down the ideas you conceive during these critical moments and use them as the basis for future reflections. Before you realize it, these ideas have developed into a fully-fledged vision. Self-reflection is a vital lifestyle for most successful people, and practicing it consistently has immeasurable benefits to your total development. It is indeed a true vision trigger.

5. KNOWLEDGE

The essence of vision conception through reading is the encounter with knowledge or colliding with understanding. Many visions have been conceived through the acquisition of knowledge or understanding. Sometimes, reading or studies expose us to either a problem or a potential solution to an existing problem. It is said that the wisdom of the ages is hidden in books. In books lie many discoveries that are yet to be implemented, ideas that are yet to be developed, solutions that are yet to be implemented, and visions, dreams, goals that are yet to be realized. The more you read, the more you encounter and amass knowledge and the higher the probability of creating a conducive environment for vision conception and growth. However, there is no correlation between knowledge and vision; there are highly educated individuals who have no vision, and the opposite is true as well. Notwithstanding, knowledge is one of the triggers of vision.

Some ministers have conceived vision for their churches through the words of scripture. Napoleon Hill's book *Think and Grow Rich* has triggered many wealth creation visions, Dale Carnegie's books have created countless visions on effective public speaking, and John Maxwell's books have generated numerous visions on leadership. The bottom line is that knowledge exposed by great books are potential triggers of visions. Those who find time to engage in the text of such books stand a better chance of conceiving, nurturing, growing, and realizing great visions. Most of such visions are soulish, since they reside in the intellect and are generated from your will. I have no doubt that the text of this book will trigger the conception of many visions for its readers, help many to refine and develop their existing visions, and direct others to the path of success. Knowledge in any form is a potential trigger of vision!

The realization of soulish visions has brought profound change and transformation to the lives of many people on multiple fronts. The fulfillment of great soulish visions is proof that one does not have to be a spiritual person to conceive and realize your true vision in life. If you have a soul, you can be a visionary. Today, I call upon leaders to subject themselves to clear, impactful, and transformative visions. Soulish visions usually do not directly promote the advancement of the kingdom of God, but some of them are essential for the furtherance of humanity and may indirectly impact the work of the kingdom of God. Technological innovations, medical breakthroughs, academic discoveries, architectural adventures, and many visions that have resulted in the progress of humanity were born out of the soul. Soulish visions are essential and may be complementary to spiritual visions.

Chapter Summary

- Soulish vision: This is the type of vision conceived in the soul of an individual. This type of vision can be conceived through will, emotions, and intellect.

- The following are some triggers of soulish vision: necessity, planning, experience, self-reflection, and knowledge.

- Necessity is the mother of invention, planning provides a reality of scope, experiences provide perspective and alternative. self-reflection provides opportunity for introspection, and knowledge offers the platform for problem or solution discovery.

CHAPTER FOUR

SPIRITUAL VISION

("When you have a sense of your own identity and a vision of where you want to go in life, you then have the basis for reaching out to the world and going after your dreams for a better life."
-Stedman Graham)

> *"And it shall come to pass afterward, that I will pour out my spirit upon all flesh; and your sons and your daughters shall prophesy, your old men shall dream dreams, your young men shall see visions."*
>
> **Joel 2:28 NKJV**

VISION STORY-WILLIAM WILBERFORCE

William Wilberforce, the man accredited for ending the slave trade in most of the British Empire, had a huge vision. On October 28, 1787, he wrote out his one-liner vision: "God Almighty has set before me two great objects, the suppression of the slave trade and the reformation of morals." That was a fearful and intimidating vision conceived by William Wilberforce. The business of slave trade was so lucrative at the time that any thought of it being abolished would have been met with fearful opposition. Certainly, this vision seemed impossible and just ridiculous. But guess what? It took forty-six years, but it happened. Wilberforce saw slavery abolished in almost the entirety of the British Empire three days before he went to be with the Lord for eternity. He worked his entire life towards the realization of this vision, and it certainly happened.

INTRODUCTION

―◆◆◆―

"Spiritual visions are usually bigger and more profound than the vision-bearer and their perceived capabilities."

―◆◆◆―

Spiritual vision, the third type of vision, is conceived in the realms of the spirit, revealed through the Holy Spirit, and manifested through a spiritual person. In the Bible, the word vision is more often used as an encounter with God where He imparts special revelation, intuition, or in dreams (Numbers 12:6). Sometimes visions can be theophanies, where God speaks directly to the visionary (Numbers 12:8). Spiritual visions are typically bigger and more profound than the vision-bearer and their perceived capacities. The scripture above (Joel 2:28) indicates the dependency of spiritual visions on the presence of the Spirit of God. God indicated that upon the arrival of His Spirit, recipients would have the enablement for spiritual visions.

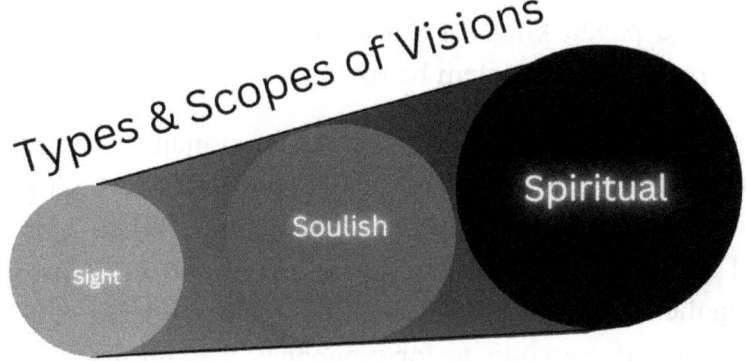

Manifestation of Spiritual Vision

Though God is never changing, as written in Malachi 3:6 NIV, "I am the Lord, and I do not change...", He works in dynamic ways to reveal the future state of individuals, groups and nations. He does this for His glorification and for the benefit of His people in order to either prepare, warn, save or redeem them.

Though God is omnipotent, omniscient, and omnipresent, the implementation of some visions is dependent on man because he was given dominion over the Earth (Genesis 1:28 NIV). Once man agrees to cooperate and collaborate with God's vision, nothing can stop its manifestation. As much as Satan whispers in the ears of believers trying to convince them that they cannot implement the vision of God, he is WRONG, just like in the beginning of creation. Age, gender, nationality, ethnicity, physical strength, intelligence quotient (IQ), and financial status are not limitations to the manifestation of spiritual visions, because God is limitless. He is able to use whomever He deems worthy, despite what the world may say. Examples include Elizabeth, who despite her very advanced age brought forth John the Baptist (Luke 1 NIV). Prophetess Deborah delivered the Nation of Israel (Judges 4, 5 NIV). Gideon won the battle against the Midianites, despite being the least in his family from the weakest clan in the smallest tribe (Judges 6 NIV). Cyprus the Great (a pagan king) of the Medes-Persian Empire, decreed that the Temple of Jerusalem be rebuilt (Isaiah 44:28 NIV).

As God is not constrained to the nature of man to manifest His Vision, neither is spiritual vision; it is not dependent on natural forces but transcends through multiple realms. When Mary was visited by Archangel Gabriel, who informed her of the prospects of being the mother of the Messiah, she was bewildered. She knew that the natural prerequisite for pregnancy was intimacy, but she was a virgin. Gabriel had to teach her that the manifestation of supernatural vision is not dependent on the fulfillment of natural factors. As Mary was called, maybe God is calling you for a special assignment, but you are focused on the fulfillment of some natural events, factors, and requirements. I want to encourage you to permit a paradigm shift in your thought process and focus your attention on the God of the supernatural and allow His vision to manifest in your life through faith; "for we walk by faith, not by sight." 2 Corinthians 5:7 NKJV.

Further examples of spiritual visions are noted in the lives of Simeon and Moses. In the book of Luke chapter 2, Simeon, a righteous and devout priest from Jerusalem, did not allow death to prevent him from seeing the Messiah and the consolation of Israel. When Mary and Joseph brought Jesus to the Temple to perform the redemption of the firstborn in accordance with the Law, Simeon took Jesus into his arms and said, "Sovereign Lord, as you have promised, you may now dismiss your servant in peace. For my eyes have seen your salvation, which you have prepared in the sight of all nations: a light for revelation to the Gentiles, and the glory of your people Israel." Luke 2:25-32. Simeon was so convinced about the vision of seeing the Savior of the world that he resisted the power of death until the realization of the vision. His vision brought the "time clock to a standstill," preventing him from experiencing death, halting his biological degeneration until the realization of the vision. This is an example of an unwavering strong vision that defied all odds, including basic biological functions of an organism. The abilities of strong visions are just beyond imagination. Simeon developed an impeccable resilience in his body to resist and postpone the power of death until the vision became a reality. Not only did Simeon see Jesus Christ, but he also held him. The vision of the Savior became tangible to him, a full realization.

In the case of Moses, his vision seemed impossible against the backdrop of Egypt's military prowess, one of the most powerful empires at that time. His vision was not only to liberate the Jewish people from Egyptian enslavement, but also to take them to the Promised Land. Though the vision was definitely from the spiritual realms and commanded by God, it did not occur without moments of discouragement. One of these moments was that though Moses had been obedient to the call, he would not see the Promised Land due to his inability to handle provocation from his followers. In Deuteronomy 34, the Lord showed Moses on Mount Nebo the vision of the Promised Land, but then informed him that "…but thou shalt not go over thither. So, Moses the servant of the Lord died there in the land of Moab, according to the word of the Lord." Deuteronomy 34: 5 NKJV. He was not discouraged by the fact that he would not see the Promised Land. Instead, he was encouraged because the vision was not about his selfish needs but the needs of Israel, the covenant between God and His people and His glorification. After thousands of years, on the Mount of Transfiguration, Moses' vision of going to the Promised Land became a reality when he appeared to Jesus Christ along with the Prophet Elijah. See Mark 9:2–8 NIV, Matthew 17:1–8 NIV, and Luke 9:28–36 NIV. His vision outlived him, just as all spiritual visions have the power to outlive their earthly bearers.

Chapter Summary

- Spiritual visions originate from the realm of the spirit, channeled through the spirit and manifested through a spiritual person.

- Spiritual visions are usually bigger and more profound than the conceiver.

- Although God is omnipotent, omnipresent, and omniscient, He still uses the agency of man to bring His vision into reality.

- As long as man cooperates and collaborates with God, nothing can stop the manifestation of spiritual vision.

- Natural elements such as age, gender, nationality, physical appearance or strength, intelligent quotient (IQ) etc., do not determine the manifestation of spiritual vision.

- It takes faith to bring spiritual vision into reality.

- Spiritual visions mostly outlive their bearers.

CHAPTER FIVE

THE NATURE AND CHARACTERISTICS OF VISION (PART 1)

("Vision is the art of seeing what is invisible to others"
- Jonathan Swift)

He said, "Listen to my words: 'When there is a prophet among you, I, the Lord, reveal myself to them in visions, I speak to them in dreams.'"

Numbers 12:6 NIV

VISION STORY-MARK ZUCKERBERG

On October 28, 2021, in his founder's letter, Mark Zuckerberg wrote to Facebook employees the vision for the future of the company he called Meta. This letter was to position the company and prepare the minds of the employees for the upcoming metaverse, and I quote a statement from said letter: **"From now on, we will be metaverse-first, not Facebook-first. That means that over time you won't need a Facebook account to use our other services. As our new brand starts showing up in our products, I hope people around the world come to know the Meta brand and the future we stand for."** The word "meta" means beyond, and the word verse comes from the universe: "all existing matter and space considered as a whole; the cosmos." By this vision, Mark Zuckerberg has set a tone for the virtual reality future of the metaverse where a platform will enable people from all over the world to engage in meaningful conversation within a virtual reality space. Thus, the company, which started as a directory of information for college students and later became a social networking service, has now metamorphosed its vision into the creation of a virtual reality ecosystem- the metaverse.

INTRODUCTION

Vision, by nature, provides the opportunity to crystalize the future within the present. It allows entities (individuals or organizations) to separate themselves and establish their own goals irrespective of present circumstances or constraints. Characteristics of a vision are the inherent qualities that define the nature of a vision. In order to understand the true meaning of vision, the following key characteristics should be defined and explained.

1. EVERY AUTHENTIC VISION IS UNIQUE

Every authentic vision is unique in its context and composition despite any obvious similarities; this is irrespective of the individual, organization, or denomination. No two visions are the same. The uniqueness of every vision can be expressed in terms of its strengths, values, directions, beliefs, and outputs. Every vision is unique because it is without equal, and may be unusual or very remarkable. The idea of uniqueness is true even in ministry. No two ministries are the same no matter how similar they may appear. The responsibilities and tasks in God's business are so vast that no individual or denomination can amass enough capabilities to accomplish them all. Therefore, God has given each one a unique ministerial vision to pursue. If you have not yet identified your ministerial vision, continue to pray and the God who called you will unveil it to you.

"The uniqueness of every vision ensures that it is devoid of competition and comparison."

The uniqueness of vision ensures that they are devoid of competition and comparison. This is why it is imperative to embrace the uniqueness of one's own vision, which may be the source of its strength. Comparing visions leads to rushed decisions, dissatisfaction in life, and thoughts of inadequacy. Comparisons extract inner motivation, leaving little or no hope when measured against those who may seem to be ahead in life. If the vision is original and unique, then the challenges, experiences and opportunities will have no equal.

One of the reasons why one compares is insecurity, and that insecurity is rooted in fear. Fear is due to the feeling that one does not have the intelligence, appearance, personality, finances, or ability to accomplish the vision. These feelings are against the knowledge and Word of God, and need to be brought into captivity and the obedience of Christ (2 Corinthians 10:5 NIV). Scripture has already stated that believers are "fearfully and wonderfully made" (Psalms 139:14 NIV); "For God hath not given us the spirit of fear; but of power, and of love, and of a sound mind" (2 Timothy 1:7 NIV); "Do not be anxious about anything…" (Philippians 4:6 NIV)"; and "Each one should test their own actions. Then they can take pride in themselves alone, without comparing themselves to someone else, for each one should carry their own load." (Galatians 6:4-5 NIV). Even God told Peter not to compare when he had inquired about John's mission (John 21:22 NIV).

Therefore, embrace your own vision and run your unique race. Be unique and original, knowing that the photocopy can never surpass the original in beauty. Along with not comparing the actual vision, do not compare the execution of the vision, because no matter how similar they may look, the content, context, composition, and completion are never the same. Yes, it is important to learn from others' mistakes, but make room for your failures, setbacks, and disappointments; this is a necessary part of the journey. Focusing on the vision diminishes the time allowed for competing or comparing to others, while permitting more time and effort to be used for establishing and accomplishing the vision.

2. VISION RESTRICTS/RESTRAINS

"The lives, decisions and relationships of a visionary are guided and merged to a tapestry towards the realization of the vision."

Vision restricts the bearers for the purpose of its fulfillment: visionaries usually do not have the liberty to live any way they like. Their lives, decisions, and relationships are guided, merging to form a tapestry towards the realization of the vision. The burden of realizing the vision will restrict one's actions and thoughts. The spectrum of a visionary's decision-making and choices is limited to areas that will promote the attainment of the vision. The value of living a restricted life is such that the vision will constrain you to only the essentials, which are the will, the way, and the wishes of God and the bearer. This is like the work of the gospel. Scripture expresses the liberation of the gospel only through the attainment of a Christ like character. The Christ-like character emboldens the visionary to be vision-oriented and heed wisdom, while others without those characteristics and vision cast off restraints, such as those found in Proverbs 29:18.

Vision defines the boundaries to live by and restrains life to fit within those boundaries. It strengthens the believer to say no to temptation and sin and creates a necessary spiritual tunnel towards Christ in this loud and chaotic world. Moreover, it provides direction, momentum, and at times an anchor. Without limitations or boundaries, it is easy to needlessly drift into the sea of death and distraction. Without direction, it is easy to travel on the wrong path. Without momentum, it is easy to remain stagnant. Without an anchor, it is easy to be distracted or carried away by the storms of life. A vision-focused believer is like the Apostle Paul, who stated in Galatians 2:20 NIV, that "I have been crucified with Christ and I no longer live, but Christ lives in me." The visionary no longer lives, but the vision lives through him. It has the power to subdue and "kill" earthly will, desires, ways, and wishes. He no longer lives for himself but for the manifestation and glorification of the vision. This is the restrictive nature of vision. Seize the rare opportunity of living for a vision and the satisfaction and fulfillment will be beyond your imagination.

3. VISION PROMOTES SELF-DISCIPLINE

Vision creates a circumference for self-discipline. All matters that do not cultivate the vision become a waste of precious time. Such focus fosters self-discipline, which allows the visionary to subjugate their emotions, desires, and will for the manifestation of the vision. This subjugation is not just some effortless and painless action, but an act that can at times be daunting and tough. It spans from the moment of being awake to the moment of deep sleep. It affects time and budget management, social media usage, behavior, conversations with friends, sleep schedule, and even food consumption. When a vision is conceived, the passionate desire towards its achievement creates a circumference of self-discipline. No visionary wastes time on unnecessary, unproductive activities or engagements.

4. VISION SEPARATES

Vision separates the bearer from the masses and may at times create an atmosphere of loneliness needed for its development and manifestation. The crystallization of certain visions requires the removal of all sources of interference and distraction. Separation may provide the right environment to analyze, question oneself, identify potential challenges and risk factors, discover possible alternative paths to success, and fully comprehend the magnitude of the vision and its success indicators. Therefore, visionaries must intentionally learn to embrace and enjoy solitude. Times of solitude must therefore be used productively to ensure that the vision is well accessed before it starts encountering challenges, oppositions, and competitions. Some visions have not materialized because the bearers did not have ample time of assessment before implementation. Those who do not have enough time to assess their vision but rush to implementation are sometimes stunned by the potential challenges they encounter on the path to realization. Such surprises are the results of lack of proper preparation, an essential process achieved during the time of separation.

THE NATURE AND CHARACTERISTICS OF VISION (PART 1)

"Vision liberates the visionary from being unproductively busy to being focused and effective."

Vision liberates the visionary from being unproductively busy to being focused and effective; some people are so busy but achieve very little. Being busy does not mean being successful; success is a measure of achievement, not engagement. One can engage all day and night, but in the end, it is the achievements that matter. Vision may separate and prepare the visionary to better channel their energy and effort into achievable tasks. Therefore, the time of separation is not a wasted time but invested time meant to yield positive dividends.

In addition to creating self-discipline and focus, vision separates and quarantines for purging. Purging is part of the preparation. There are instances where people have conceived visions but may not be ready emotionally, psychologically, socially, or spiritually for its implementation. The purpose of self-quarantine is to purge any behavioral and character excesses that may hinder the proper development of the vision. This process not only creates opportunities for implementing the vision effectively but also allows a more conducive character to be formed.

5. VISION EVOLVES

Most visions evolve with time. Sometimes God will not reveal the totality of the vision at the onset. He does this not because He does not trust His children's ability but because He knows how easily intimidation, fear, and doubt can take root, leading to the abandonment of the vision. To avoid any potential derailments, God usually dispenses the vision in bits and pieces. By doing this, the vision-bearer gradually pursues the vision without becoming overwhelmed. Yes, the pursuit of every great vision can be very overwhelming at times, but evolutionary revelation presents a greater opportunity for management on the path to its realization. 1 Corinthians 13: 9-10 NIV indicates that "For we know in part and we prophesy in part, but when completeness comes, what is in part disappears." The progressive revelation of God's vision and knowledge is a strategic way of managing the vision-bearer's expectation. Details of this attribute will come to life in later chapters.

Even most soulish visions also evolve over time. The visionaries may not have the full scope at the unset, but as it transitions through the phases of growth and development, the scope of the vision begins to widen and the details are unearthed. For most visions, the scope at implementation is much wider and bigger than at conception. So no matter how small your vision may be, do not despise the beginning of little things. It is only a matter of time until such vision may broaden beyond your imagination. Pursue every little vision whilst allowing the infusion of bigger dimensions on the path to implementation.

6. VISION ATTRACTS ENEMIES

"See, the enemy is puffed up; his desires are not upright but the righteous person will live by his faithfulness." (Habakkuk 2:4 NIV)

Vision easily attracts enemies. In this fallen world, society unfortunately desires the effortless way to wealth, prosperity, and fame. Many are willing to accept the end state of popularity but are not ready to put in the required level of investment and sacrifice. Because of this, many unguarded hearts are prone to envy and jealousy. It is not uncommon for vision-bearers to attract enemies, knowingly or unknowingly. Some people are unable to control themselves, especially when they would rather be the ones receiving the recognition for achieving their visions. Sometimes, such enemies will construct strategies of distraction or may throw in challenges meant to impede progress. All too often, people proclaim baseless accusations or lies against people of vision. Do not be alarmed if those vision assassins are "friends" or "loved ones." Despite attracting enemies or animosities against the vision, it is imperative to continue to be steadfast and immovable in its pursuit.

It is not a coincidence that right after the Lord instructed the Prophet to write the vision down in Habakkuk 2:2-3, the next verse commences with the attitude of the enemy. To say "the enemy is puffed up; his desires are not upright" (Habakkuk 2:4 NIV) indicates the distractive behavior of the enemy against the vision. So yes, the Lord may have given the vision, but the enemy works to thwart or abort it. In this scripture, the Lord was creating awareness of the existence and possible attack of the enemy against the vision given to the prophet. Do not be naïve enough to think that God's given visions are immune from the attacks of the enemy. Protecting the vision from either spiritual enemies or vulnerable humans is vital to bringing it to a reality. Sometimes the level of protection may involve keeping mute as exhibited by Mary (Luke 2:19 NKJV) or practicing selective sharing. Be careful who is allowed to know of the vision, because not everyone will be genuinely happy or willing to support your vision. Learn to identify and avoid the dream killers, the vision assassins, the hope snatchers and stealers, for the devil is looking for opportunities to steal visions.

Examples of the devil trying to kill visions include the attempted elimination of Joseph in the Bible by his brothers and his subsequent enslavement in Egypt, assassinations of Dr. Martin Luther King Jr and President John F. Kennedy, and the overthrow of Dr. Kwame Nkrumah, the first president of Ghana. Joseph's vision of leadership and rulership was a threat to his visionless brothers, who were so content with watching over their father's sheep. Dr. Martin Luther King Jr's. vision of utilizing the power of words, acts of nonviolent resistance, and civil disobedience to achieve seemingly impossible goals and effect social change was a force to be reckoned with and a threat to his enemies. President John F Kennedy's vision of revolutionizing human rights and restoring civil rights in America at the time the United States was drowning with multiple domestic and international crises was not going to proceed unnoticed. His assassination was not solely against the person but more so against his vision. Besides Dr. Kwame Nkrumah blowing the trumpet of political change and liberation across Africa, his strategic alliance and economic development agenda were unceasing sources of worry and threat to the enemies of the continent. The overthrow of Dr. Kwame Nkrumah's government was an attempt to murder his vision.

In conclusion, when it comes to vision, always remember that the enemy is puffed up and his desires are not upright. The vision assassins are always lurking and looking for an opportunity to strike. Handle your visions with care, especially during the formative stages, and guard them against unnecessary exposure.

THE NATURE AND CHARACTERISTICS OF VISION (PART 1)

Chapter Summary

Characteristics of a vision are the inherently distinguishing features that define its nature. Understanding characteristics provides a better opportunity to comprehend the topic of vision and create a framework for its implementation.

1. Every Authentic Vision is Unique: Every authentic vision is unique in its composition, context, content and completion. The uniqueness of a vision ensures that it is devoid of competition and comparison.

2. Vision Restricts/Restrains: Vision restricts the bearer for the purpose of its fulfillment. The lives, decisions, and relationships of the visionaries are guided while the burden of its realization restricts their actions and thoughts.

3. Vision Promotes Self-Discipline: Vision creates a circumference for self-discipline and causes the visionaries to focus their emotions, desires, and wills for its manifestation.

4. Vision Separates: Vision separates the bearer from the masses and may create an atmosphere of loneliness. The crystallization of certain visions requires the removal of any potential source of interference or distraction.

5. Vision Evolves: Most visionaries may not comprehend the full scope of the vision at the onset, but as it transitions through the phases of growth and development, the scope of the vision begins to widen and the details are unearthed. For most visions, the scope at implementation is much wider and bigger than at conception.

6. Vision Attracts Enemies: Vision easily attracts enemies. This fallen world has opened the hearts of many to jealousy and envy, as seen in people's willingness to accept a

state of popularity without commensurate investment and sacrifice.

CHAPTER SIX

THE NATURE AND CHARACTERISTICS OF VISION (PART II)

("Action without vision is only passing time. Vision without action is merely daydreaming. But vision with action can change the world." – Nelson Mandela)

The boy Samuel ministered before the Lord under Eli. In those days the word of the Lord was rare; there were not many visions.

1 Samuel 3:1 (NIV)

VISION STORY- MICHAEL JORDAN

Michael Jordan, born on February 17, 1963, is a billionaire American businessman and former professional basketball player. According to the National Basketball Association (NBA) official website, "by acclamation, Michael Jordan is the greatest basketball player of all time." His impressive professional basketball career spanned a duration of fifteen seasons in the NBA between 1984 and 2003, winning six NBA championships with the Chicago Bulls. His individual achievements and accolades include six NBA Finals Most Valuable Player (MVP) awards, ten NBA scoring titles (both all-time records), five NBA MVP awards, ten All-NBA First Team designations, nine All-Defensive First Team honors, fourteen NBA All-Star Game selections, three NBA All-Star Game MVP awards, three NBA steals titles, and the 1988 NBA Defensive Player of the Year Award. He holds the NBA records for career regular season scoring average (30.1 points per game) and career playoff scoring average (33.4 points per game).

All these accolades had been met with great objection when his try out for the basketball varsity team during his sophomore year of high school was unsuccessful, as he was deemed too short to play with a height of 5 feet 11 inches (1.80 m). Fueled by his vision and motivated to prove his worth, he trained vigorously, gained acceptance the following summer (after growing additional four inches) and became the star of Laney's junior varsity team. Great visions are worth every effort, though people may not see your vision at the onset.

1. PEOPLE MAY NOT SEE YOUR VISION

Not everyone has the capacity to see or understand an assigned vision. Vision is not birthed in a vacuum; there are certain prerequisites that must be fulfilled to create the right environment for its conception. Those who have not developed the right set of conditions, such as conducive mindset, right spiritual composition and standing, may not be capable of comprehending your vision even if you try to explain it to them. Nevertheless, this should not dismay the vision-bearer or cause confusion because some others just do not have what it takes. In Acts 9, the vision of Saul that led to his conversion was not seen by any of his companions though they were around. If Saul depended on those around him to see, understand, and confirm his vision, rather than trusting in his God-given discernment, who knows what would have become of the church. This is why it is important to stop trying to convince everyone to onboard your vision when they do not have the capacity or the insight to do so. Allowing others' opinions and critiques to overrule God's plan will only lead to disaster. It is against this backdrop that many visionaries have been branded insane and called all sorts of names. Some people have been waiting for validation or approval from so-called "mentors," friends, and family members before embarking on their visionary journey. Some have abandoned their visions because they did not receive the anticipated validation. Others have recoiled into their shells of disappointment due to lack of the expected support. The mistake of waiting for such an attestation is that it may never be received. God does not make mistakes; if He has provided the vision that means that the vision-bearer is the ideal temple for its gestation, growth, and realization. It is imperative not to wait for society to validate your vision before pursuing it. The green light to pursue your vision should come from either God or yourself. This is in contrast to corporate or institutional vision, which require colleagues' support for implementation and must always be shared for the necessary buy-in before implementation.

Pertaining to individual vision, support is from God, the visionary, and those whom God has assigned as allies. Only God and possibly the vision-bearer are aware of the skills, talents, and allies needed to accomplish the vision, like Paul, of whom the Lord stated, "he is a chosen vessel of mine to bear my name before Gentiles, kings, and the children of Israel. For I will show him how many things he must suffer for my name's sake." (Acts 9:15-16 NIV). Paul's ministerial pursuit was significantly different from the other apostles, as expressed in the verse above. Inherent in Paul's ministerial vision was an act of suffering, gravitation towards the gentiles, kings, and the children of Israel. Nobody else was cut out for this! Paul would have made a huge mistake in trying to carve a ministry after the pattern of Peter or any other apostle. By virtue of this vision, God had prepared Paul with the right combination of background, education, career, and experience for engaging gentiles, kings, and the children of Israel while bearing the pain of ministerial suffering. Nobody else could see this vision like Paul.

2. EVERY VISION HAS ITS PROVISION

"Divine providence is assured for the realization of every vision."

Divine providence is assured for every vision. At times, visionaries focus on what they do not have rather than what they do have, allowing their fear of possible failure to grow. Focusing on their inabilities, lack of skills or experiences only suppresses the willingness and even the desire to start developing their potential. Most visionaries do not amass their full resources before commencing their pursuit. God does not check their bank account or pocketbook before giving the vision. As earthly wealth and riches do not limit God, neither is His vision limited. It is unwise to wait for an earthly sponsor before embarking on any visionary journey, because it may never happen or may delay the timeline of vision implementation. Sometimes you just have to make a move and the provisions will be unearthed along the way.

MY VISION STORY

As a young man, I conceived a vision to further my education in the United States of America. I was accepted into a master's level business administration program (MBA Finance & Investment) but the semester tuition fee was prohibitive, since I had to pay everything out of pocket as an international student. Without a scholarship, the achievement of that vision seemed impossible at first. I was already concerned about the possible financial constraints when a dear family member reminded me ,"If we sell all the family property, we will still not have enough funds to pay for your school fees." However, the vision was so crystal clear, deep, and compelling that I refused to pay any attention to the lack of funds. I embarked on a daring journey from Ghana to the United States, with one small carryon bag and a few dollar bills, not knowing how my education was going to be funded. After persistent pursuit of the vision, I graduated and was awarded a master's degree in the aforementioned subject.

In between my arrival and graduation, there were a series of difficulties and challenges, including working two full time hard-labor jobs and one part time job, in addition to enrollment as a full-time student concurrently. Some setbacks included being expelled from class for non-payment of tuition fees, registering the minimum classes per semester just to manage the amount of fees to be paid, and many more that will be shared at the appropriate time. My setback stories are many, but eventually it was my comeback story that prevailed. It still beats my imagination anytime I reminisce on how my education was funded, but I can only attribute it to divine providence. God's provision is always in the vision. God will give you a vision as a means of His provision.

Be Encouraged

I want to encourage you to look beyond what you have or do not have. If the Lord is with you, His provision is assured in your life. Yes, sometimes it may be difficult; like in the case of

Abraham, the initial manifestation of your Promised Land may not be flowing with milk and honey. This may cause you to travel to Egypt to seek for greener pastures, but I can assure you that if you do not give up and continue to depend on Jehovah Jireh, He will provide all your needs for the fulfillment of the vision. So go on, shake away your inadequacies, inabilities, and insufficiencies, chase after the vision, and you will soon see it manifesting in your life. Your provision is right there staring at you from your vision.

3. VISION REQUIRES FAITH

Every human being has a fundamental level of faith called natural faith. We employ this in our daily lives; however, sometimes we need supernatural faith to ensure that we do and achieve things that may seem a bit difficult or impossible. By natural faith, you know that you will wake up the following day after going to bed, cross over the ocean to your destination when traveling by airplane, receive healing upon taking medications prescribed by the doctor, quench your thirst upon drinking water, and have the needed nutrients for living when you eat. All these are exhibitions of natural faith. In some instances, people do not even realize that they are employing faith in their daily lives. Depending on the type and magnitude of the vision, sometimes natural faith may suffice for its execution or realization. In other instances, however, a supernatural faith may be needed to believe in and bring the vision to fruition. The more unrealistic the vision is, the more faith is needed for its execution.

When corporate executives meet to devise a vision strategy for their organization, they are inherently exhibiting faith. Authors employ faith when they pen down their first word to author a book. Students' exhibit natural faith when they enroll in an academic institution to pursue a degree program. Prospective couples em-

THE NATURE AND CHARACTERISTICS OF VISION (PART II)

ploy faith to commence their life journey together. Therefore, you realize that faith is part of our daily life. However, there are some visions that will not be realized with natural faith. Every type or form of vision will require a certain level of faith for its realization. Without faith, the smallest vision will not be realized.

The Bible gives a definition of faith in Hebrews 11:1-6 and proceeds to recount certain visions that were achieved through the eyes of faith. Whether it is the acceptable sacrifice of Abel, the resilience of Abraham to have an offspring even at an old age, the grace upon which Enoch escaped a taste of death, or the acceptance of Mary as a channel for the birth of the Messiah, they all boil down to faith. These biblical patriarchs and matriarchs had supernatural faith in order to bring their supernatural visions to reality. We, as God's children led by the Holy Spirit, also have the ability to operate with this supernatural faith; we just need to tap into and develop it. We have been called and given different dimensions of God's vision. If the vision appears too big, rely on the arms of faith, knowing that faith is indeed the evidence of things not seen. It is only a matter of time before the substance of things hoped for will become a reality.

4. VISION GENERATES INSPIRATION AND MOTIVATION

Deuteronomy 31:6 NIV ~ "Be strong and courageous. Do not fear or be in dread of them, for it is the Lord your God who goes with you. He will not leave you or forsake you."

Vision speaks to the inner being of the bearer and can generate positive emotions or energy. Due to the many challenges and obstacles that a vision may face during its growth, it is essential that vision-bearers are inspired or motivated for its achievement. Vision is a source of inspiration. The passion or desire to achieve the results generates an inner energy or force to propel the visionary above challenges, obstacles, hurdles, or difficulties. This internal energy is the cause of the relentless pursuit experienced by most visionaries. If your vision is not strong enough to propel you forward, then the vision is not compelling enough for execution.

Many people find it easier to progress towards achieving their goals by external motivation. Of course, we are all motivated when we have cheerleaders around us. In contrast, visionaries are inspired and motivated by the passion to succeed. Yes, motivation from other people may surface every now and then; however, that is not a primary factor, it is a differentiation factor. I mentioned earlier that sometimes vision would separate you from the masses. The ability to inspire oneself is the key success factor during the time of separation and loneliness. This ability is born out of what feeds the soul: willpower, emotional attachment, intelligence, and focus of the mind. Visionaries should have strong willpower for success, develop their emotional intelligence, and carry a sense of optimism. These factors fuel an internal combustion to generate the needed energy for propelling the vision forward. Additionally, the consistent focus on what you may become, the level of influence you may exert, the number of lives you may transform positively, the professional position you may attain, the neighborhood in which you may reside, the family dynamics you may change or achieve, the opportunities you may provide for your children and others with the realization of the vision may trigger a continuous and sustained inspiration.

Arise and craft your vision. Meditate and brood over the vision. Digest and assimilate the vision. Fuse the vision into your daily life. Sleep and wake up with your vision. Cry and laugh with your vision. Let your vision be so much ingrained in you that you give yourself no option but to succeed. Once you arrive at this stage, you will build enough motivation and inspiration to overcome every obstacle or difficulty on your path to vision fulfillment.

5. VISION GIVES STRENGTH FOR ENDURANCE

Jeremiah 29:11 NIV ~ "'For I know the plans I have for you,' declares the Lord, 'plans to prosper you and not to harm you, plans to give you hope and a future.'"

Proverbs 3:5-6 NIV ~ "Trust in the Lord with all your heart, and do not lean on your own understanding. In all your ways acknowledge him, and he will make straight your paths."

The concept of strength endurance is highly visible in the field of sports. It is defined as requiring "... a relatively long duration of muscle tension with minimal decrease in efficiency" (Stiff 2000). Endurance in the field of vision is the ability to maintain consistent performance towards the achievement of the vision. Strength endurance is needed to maintain an optimal level of performance over a long duration without cutting corners. The duration between a vision's conception until its realization may be incredibly significant. In addition, some visions may encounter an appreciable level of challenges, difficulties, and obstacles before they are realized. This calls for the development of psychological, emotional, intellectual, and sometimes spiritual (for spiritual visions) endurance.

A well-conceived vision develops an internal strength that provides stability and endurance. Against the duration and difficulties, endurance is essential on the path to realization of the vision. If you do not develop the art of endurance, you will never have what you ought to have and will never be who you ought to be. A key success factor for the realization of your vision is the ability to endure. Once you maintain yourself on the path of motion, it is only a matter of time before you arrive at your destination. In other words, if you continue to move forward despite the obstacles, eventually you will build the endurance needed for completion.

> *"A well-conceived vision develops internal strength for stability and endurance."*

Some people have abandoned their vision because they had a wrong judgment on its duration. You may be asking yourself, why is it taking so long for me to arrive? You feel like quitting because your vision has tarried for too long. Alternatively, the difficulties and obstacles on the path are weighing you down. You are not alone; indeed, longevity, difficulties, and obstacles are some of the main reasons for abandonment of vision. Nevertheless, I am here to encourage you to refocus and keep your eye on the vision. Continue to see yourself in that position, as that wife or husband, the godly parent raising godly children, the non-corrupt African politician, the owner of that business, the CEO of that company, the minister who leads his church members with the truth, and the agent of change in that society. Always remember that "the vision is yet for an appointed time...though it tarries; wait for it; because it will surely come." (Habakkuk 2:3 NIV). This is the assurance you have, that no matter how long it takes, it will be realized if you maintain the path of continuity and consistency. Your endurance hinges on the assurance that it will surely come. Yes! It will surely come, so go back and embrace that abandoned vision, recalibrate yourself, allow that paradigm shift, and relentlessly pursue your vision. You have what it takes, and I am sure it is for a time like this that you have been placed in that family, community, nation, and the world.

THE NATURE AND CHARACTERISTICS OF VISION (PART II)

Chapter Summary

- People May Not See Your Vision: Not everyone has the capacity to see or understand your vision. Vision is not birthed in a vacuum, but rather needs the presence of certain elements for its conception, growth, and realization. Those without the required inherent elements may not be able to comprehend your vision. Bearers of individual visions should not wait for validation or attestation from others before their vision pursuit.

- Every Vision Has its Provision: There is provision for every vision. Divine providence is assured for bearers of spiritual vision while soulish visionaries must also be assured of the provision in the vision.

- Vision Requires Faith: Every vision requires either natural or supernatural faith for its realization. The more unrealistic the vision, the greater the amount of faith needed to bring it into a reality.

- Vision Generates Inspiration and Motivation: Every vision produces an intrinsic energy that fuels and propels the bearer above any obstacle or challenge. This fuel serves as a source of inspiration and motivation.

- Vision Gives Strength for Endurance: Endurance, as it pertains to vision, is the ability to maintain consistent performance, assurance, and focus towards its achievement.

CHAPTER SEVEN

PHASES OF VISION

("It is a terrible thing to see and have no vision"-Helen Keller)

"For the vision is yet for an appointed time, but at the end it shall speak, and not lie: though it tarry, wait for it; because it will surely come, it will not tarry."

Habakkuk 2:3 NIV

VISION STORY- WALT DISNEY

The story is told of Walt Disney, who envisioned building the greatest vacation kingdom of the world in 1960. Construction work to bring the vision of Disney World into reality began on May 30, 1967, and the resort opened on October 1, 1971. Although Walt Disney died on December 15, 1966, his vision of creating this kingdom outlived him and that vision became a reality on October 1, 1971. Today, that vision still lives on, as many people, both young and old, visit Disney World in Orlando, Florida to experience the happiest times of their lives. The vision has become a reality and continues to live on decades after the demise of the vision-bearer.

INTRODUCTION

The Lord told the Prophet that there is an appointed time for the fulfillment of a vision and that is different from the time of conception. The serious consequence of a visionless individual or society is expressed in the first part of Proverbs 29:18 NIV; "where there is no vision, the people perish." I will discuss the topic of visionless in the subsequent chapter. However even when there is vision, the bearer must understand that every vision goes through multiple phases before it is realized or fulfilled. As indicated in the scripture above, the prophet Habakkuk was instructed to specifically write the vision down for an appointed time. There seems to be a communication that there is a time difference between the conception of a vision and its realization. Though every vision has its timeline, it is essential to know that vision tarries; therefore, actively waiting for the realization will help the vision-bearer navigate through the phases successfully. Creating and working towards a vision can be very daunting and sometimes overwhelming because of the many moving parts. However, any vision that does not go through the proper phases of development and maturity will find its fulfillment elusive. This is because the process of development of a vision is essential to createing the needed knowledge, experience, skill, and environment for its manifestation.

The slow movement of a predator towards its prey is not an exhibition of weakness or inability but the manifestation of a calculated accuracy for success. Do not be frustrated when your vision tarries; it is for an appointed time, and it shall surely happen. Jesus developed His vision of salvation over a 30-year duration. Abraham's vision for having a son with Sarah lasted for over 25 years before it finally came to pass. It took Moses about 40 years to see into the vision of God. The vision to deliver God's people from slavery, take them through enemies' territories, challenging weather conditions, over many natural and man-made obstacles and finally unto the elusive Promised Land, was no easy task for him. Solomon spent about seven years bringing the vision of the Temple of God into a reality. It is important to mention that the timeline of every vision is unique and diverse, just as its composition.

The following are the four main overlapping phases of vision development. I shall treat a fifth exceptional phase at the end of this chapter. It is an exceptional phase because many visions do not go through that phase. Now let us look at the four main phases of vision and what each phase entails.

1. CONCEPTION PHASE

The first phase of the vision process is the conception phase. Some visions are conceived out of necessity, presence of issues or problems, planning, self-reflection, encounter with knowledge, life experiences, stumbled upon, or given by God. Conceiving the vision is just the preliminary phase of the process but it takes time to nurture, grow, and mature.

In the conception phase, the person may have a full appreciation of the problem, challenge, or need. Most people may also have a promising idea of the potential solution, but the desire to provide a solution becomes so strong that it can no longer be pushed under the carpet. This is the commencement of the restlessness that develops resilience for persistent pursuit of the future state. Some visionaries may express this as a strong, burning desire, uncommon worry, unceasing visualization, or a magnifying echo in their souls. Every conceived vision is accompanied by a fervent desire for its realization. Whether it is a vision to provide a solution to a problem, define the future state of an individual or group, work towards technological advancement or academic pursuit, your vision will push you beyond your limit.

Nehemiah's conception of a safe and secure Jerusalem is recorded: "When I heard these things, **I sat down and wept. For some days I mourned and fasted and prayed before the God of heaven.**" Nehemiah 1:4 NIV. Upon receiving the disheartening news of Israel's compromised safety and security, Nehemiah was so troubled in his spirit that he lost the ability to continue his normal way of life. Sadness took over his soul and his appetite for food evaporated. His entire soul was consumed by this predicament, resulting in the vision to return and restore safety and security to Jerusalem. For most people, the conception of a vision manifests as a heavy burden for solution, change, improvement, or the attainment of a desired future state. It is normal for your vision to trouble your soul, and the burden it generates is necessary for its sustenance. If you are carrying any such burdens, begin to re-examine yourself well and know that your subconscious womb may be conceiving a vision. There are two main types of conception.

INSTANT AND PROGRESSIVE CONCEPTION

An instant conception occurs when an encounter causes immediate visualization of a future state. Most spiritual visions are conceived instantly, whether they manifest through dreams, revelations, or impressions. On the other hand, a vision may be conceived gradually through a process of progressive unveiling. Typically, many soulish visions are conceived gradually as more information becomes available over a period of time. Therefore, even though conception is the initial phase of vision development, it could either be instant or progressive over time.

It is important to ensure that conception is complete before jumping to the next phase. One of the major errors committed by many visionaries is that they move straight to implementation, sometimes even during the process of conception. Impulsive visionaries are those who jump straight on the implementation wagon with the slightest signal of vision conception. Such people never witness the manifestation of their visions because at that stage visions are easily aborted. You must give yourself time to properly conceive your visions, grow through the preparatory phase, and mature before implementation.

Whereas soulish vision may be conceived by triggers, God is the source and giver of spiritual visions. Once your vision is clear, it must go through other phases to ensure proper assessment and preparedness before implementation. A vision that does not transition through the phases of development may face unnecessary delays and challenges, and implementation may be elusive. Once your vision is clear, written down, and properly understood, permit the vision to transition through all the other phases before the appointed time of implementation.

2. THE PREPARATORY PHASE

The second phase of the vision development process is the preparatory phase. Proper preparation for every undertaking prevents poor performance; therefore, the importance of preparation cannot be overemphasized. Once your vision is clear, you must commit yourself to the acquisition of prerequisite knowledge. Acquisition of knowledge is key for proper preparation. Many people have committed the fatal mistake of jumping onto the implementation wagon right after the conception phase. To be rightfully positioned for success, the bearer of the vision must acquire relevant knowledge. For the young people who may be reading this book, your career, marital, family, professional, self-development, ministry, etc. vision must be commensurate with the right knowledge. Investing in acquiring the right knowledge is a key success factor for proper realization. It is therefore essential to spend ample time to gain the right level of knowledge pertaining to your vision.

Many people have aborted their visions because of lack of the knowledge needed to ensure the implementation of such visions. One of the many mistakes made by young prospective ministers is their inability to patiently acquire the rightful knowledge. Vision without corresponding knowledge is just wishful thinking and has no prospects for success. Visions are not realized unexpectedly; they must be implemented with knowledge and understanding. "My people are destroyed for lack of knowledge: because thou hast rejected knowledge, I will also reject thee, that thou shalt be no priest to me: seeing thou hast forgotten the law of thy God, I will also forget thy children." Hosea 4:6 NIV

When I conceived the vision that one day my teachings on vision would take a premium position in the global marketplace of knowledge, I resorted to reading every book I could find on the topic of vision. Therefore, this book was not born out of sheer imagination, but a calculated approach of gathering knowledge, storing, interpreting, and aligning it to meet the purpose of my vision. The word "destroyed" in Hosea 4:6 does not necessarily mean the end of an existence, but could equally be interpreted as substandard or mediocre. In other words, the lack of knowledge during the preparatory stage could easily lead to the implementation of a substandard or mediocre version of the vision.

Moses, after conceiving the vision of liberating the Hebrews from the tyranny of Pharaoh, jumped straight into execution without first acquiring sufficient knowledge and skills in conflict resolution. This resulted in Moses committing a grave mistake. However, God led him to be mentored by Jethro, a Midian priest, for forty years to acquire the requisite knowledge and skills for his ministry. Jesus' pursuit of knowledge from His early age is also documented in Luke 2:41-47 NKJV. Jesus' decision to stay with the teachers at the temple after the festival attested to His preparation and readiness to gain knowledge towards His vision for humanity, though He was still omniscient. His ability to quote the right scripture when tempted by Satan (Matthew 4:1-11 NKJV; Luke 4:2-14 NKJV) was an indication of the wealth of knowledge Jesus had accumulated during His formative years. Many ministries are plagued with mistakes due to the lack of requisite knowledge. If you have conceived any vision, commit yourself to first gathering as much knowledge as possible in that area. Gathering and gaining the right knowledge will build your confidence towards execution.

Through the acquisition of knowledge, potential alternate paths of implementation can be identified. In addition, possible risks, challenges, issues, and obstacles may also be discovered.

As you gather more knowledge during the preparatory phase, you gather the arsenal to challenge yourself on the viability of the vision. Every unchallenged vision may have loose ends and may not be ready for success-bound implementation. Challenging your vision is a recommended exercise in vision development because it helps you build your problem-solving skills, a key prerequisite for the next phase. Sometimes your vision is even enhanced during the process of knowledge acquisition. In other words, there is value added to the vision, which helps to develop a more compelling reason for its fulfillment.

Herman Meinders, the founder of American Floral Services, Inc. and the main financier of the Meinders School of Business, an ultra-modern business school at Oklahoma City University, indicated to me during one of my conversations with him that he acquired so much knowledge in his industry and his competitors that he literally "knew his competitors more than they knew themselves." His remarkable success story was partly attributed to the wealth of knowledge he had accumulated in the industry and on his competitors.

The vision is the end state, but knowledge is what will help you navigate through the terrain. The road to the vision may not be straight, may come with its challenges, but with the right level of knowledge you are prepared to achieve success. If you have conceived any vision, commit yourself to acquiring the relevant knowledge to get you ready for the next phase. If your vision is in ministry, take the path of Jesus Christ and sit at the feet of teachers to learn. If you are aspiring for entrepreneurial success, venture into the business not in ignorance but well equipped with knowledge. The vision to have a successful marriage and family life must be accompanied by understanding some basic behavioral patterns of the opposite sex and knowledge of family life. If you want to succeed in life, you must at least learn some principles of life and the laws of nature. Relevant knowledge is a great tool for success.

3. THE GESTATIONAL PHASE

The gestational phase is the closest an individual or a group can get to the fulfillment of its vision. During this phase, the composition of the vision is developed, tried, and tested. Successes, failures, and disappointments are common occurrences within this phase. As uncomfortable as this process is, it is necessary. Here, learning how to handle disappointments right after successes and learning how to get stronger, wiser, and better due to those challenges is essential to the sustainability of the vision. The right environment must be present for a vision to develop properly. For example, if you are working towards a spiritual vision, maintaining a constant spiritual presence is vital for its success. Thus, those who are pregnant with a spiritual vision cannot transition to carnality because the carnal environment cannot sustain the development of spiritual vision. Such vision will be aborted once the bearer transitions from spirituality to carnality. On the other hand, a soulish vision does not need a sound spiritual presence for its fulfillment. The right environment for development of soulish vision is the emotions, will, or intellect. Therefore, a non-spiritual person may still be able to conceive, develop, and bring to realization a soulish vision. Let us review some key developments typical for the gestation phase.

Skill Development: This is where the vision-bearer receives the training needed to develop the prerequisite skills essential for handling the manifestation of the vision. I indicated that the main factor in the preparatory phase is the acquisition of prerequisite knowledge. The proper application of the knowledge is the skill essential for ensuring success during the gestational phase. You are a step closer to the realization of the vision when you learn to apply the relevant skills towards identified tasks. Many people cannot handle the manifestation of their vision at the time it is conceived. Therefore, it is essential you receive the training to generate the required skills.

Let us review the case of King David from the Bible. "So Samuel took the horn of oil and anointed him in the presence of his brothers, and from that day on the Spirit of the Lord came powerfully upon David. Samuel then went to Ramah." 1 Samuel 16:13 NIV. Through the process of anointing, David's future state was made known to him; his future as the king of Israel (the vision) was now clear, but he did not become a king immediately. After David was anointed and received the transformative power of the Spirit of the Lord, he was then taken through his training to develop the right skills for the position to which he had been anointed. Let us look at the sequence of events that equipped David with the skills needed to become undoubtedly the greatest king in the history of Israel.

The Shepherd Boy

The shepherd takes care of sheep and is responsible for their safety and well-being. In ancient times, the work of the shepherd was to keep their flock intact, protect it from predators, milk it, and guide it to market areas in time for shearing. Some key skills for successful shepherding included being tough, hardworking, humble, learning new things, having endurance, being observant, and patience. Through his work as a shepherd boy, David developed the skills of being responsible and accountable for the vulnerable, an essential skill needed to be a great king. Like the position of the king, proper skill development is required to facilitate and establish success in every vision. In addition, as discovered by David, success is only possible if God remains in the center and acts as the ultimate Shepherd. The provision, protection, and promotion received from the Lord were vital to his success. Later, David expressed his understanding of God as his shepherd when he wrote Psalm 23.

Some of you have been called and ordained into leadership positions, but God will first take you through the dirty work, the disrespected positions, the disregarded roles and responsibilities to prepare you for the ultimate position. Do not be downhearted when your vision of leadership seems to be taking you through spectatorship or subservience. Go through this position with grace, acquire every skill possible, and one day God will exalt you to the very leadership position He has ordained for you.

Service to Saul (1 Samuel 16:15-22 NKJV)

The second area of skill development for David was through his service to King Saul. David's service to King Saul was threefold. First, David was to develop the skills of servanthood needed to build humility. As a prospective king, developing the skill of servanthood was to equip him to appreciate his future servants' services. The appreciation of servanthood is a characteristic of one of the most impactful and influential types of leadership, called servant leadership style. If David was to become a great servant leader, he first needed to experience and develop the skills of servanthood. Therefore, God provided the opportunity for David to be Saul's servant. Secondly, David was also to build his spiritual fortitude as a requirement to exorcize King Saul. Through the act of exorcism, David developed his spiritual muscle for engaging in effective spiritual battle. Thirdly, David's presence in the palace was to offer him the opportunity to see what it meant to be a king. David had firsthand information and experience of kingship, participated in Saul's administration, witnessed his weaknesses and strengths, and tasted the glamor of his prospective position.

Through the acts of servanthood, spiritual development, and

seeing the totality of kingship in Saul's palace, David developed the skills of becoming a great king. All the aforementioned activities were part of David's gestation phase of the vision. David's reign as a king was remarkably successful because he patiently received ample training and developed the skills necessary before officially becoming the king of Israel.

Skill development is necessary for successful implementation of every vision. Depending on the type of vision, this phase may last from a few days to years. No matter the duration, patiently amass your skills and at the appointed time, God will display you to the world. Do not skip this phase if you desire to achieve success in your vision implementation.

The Soldier

Another form of training David received was in military and defense. As a young shepherd, David had fought lions and bears to defend his sheep in the desert. To conclude his military training, God brought him to face Goliath, the Philistine giant from Gath (I Samuel 17 NKJV). During the times of Saul and David, the Philistines were a constant source of worry and concern for the safety and security of the Israelites. They fought the Israelites on multiple occasions (1 Samuel 4:1-22 NIV; 1 Samuel 13 NIV; 1 Samuel 14:15-52 NIV; 1 Samuel 17:1-58 NIV). God knew that David needed the experience and skill of fighting and defeating the Philistines on his resume. So, guess what happened? God set David up to fight and defeat the champion of the Philistines and gain military acumen that became invaluable during his reign as king. His encounter with and defeat of Goliath was one of the heights of his training and skill development before his ascension to the throne of Israel. The courage to stand, engage, and defend Israel against every form of opposition were all testaments to his preparedness for kingship. David's anointing alone did not bring him to the vision realization immediately; it was also his readiness, which placed him to the position of prominence.

Just as it was in the days of David, God is still looking for men and women who have patiently acquired and developed the skills to fulfill the vision of God. Remember, the vision is for an appointed time; when it tarries do not sit idle. When it seems to be delaying, do not give up. When it seems to have disappeared, do not blink. Make maximum use of every opportunity available to develop yourself patiently and quietly. Then wait on God for the opportunity and the right time.

A Sojourner

The fourth means of training and skill development was through David's expedition as a sojourner. Following his encounter with and defeat of the giant warrior Goliath, David continued to undergo other forms of training through his sojourning on the desert. David's training included: enduring homelessness, hostility and wrath from his master King Saul, losing everything including his family, mutiny by his comrades, disrespect and disappointment from Naboth (Abigail's husband), pretense of madness, the grace to forgive his pursuer and the wisdom not to extend vengeance but mercy against his enemy King Saul. Through this training, David developed the skill of survival, living in need and difficulty without compromising on his integrity. Every training you receive and skill developed becomes handy and needful for the realization of the vision. Do not cut corners nor try to skip this phase to shorten the duration of the development of your vision.

Maybe you have a great vision but are constantly faced with challenges and difficulties. You may be exhausted or on the brink of giving up. I am here to tell you that your challenges and difficulties are not meant to break you down but are the essential training needed to succeed in your vision. God is training you for success. He has not abandoned you but is preparing you for the vision. Do not pity yourself; you are not a victim but are victory bound. Your assurance of victory is inherent in the very challenges and difficulties you are encountering. Remember, the higher the grade the more difficult the test. Your training is unusual because your vision is unique. It has the potential to transform not only your life but also that of others. Your vision is a mandate that will determine the destiny of generations. The life of many hangs on your vision and its realization.

Practice Your Vision

The gestation phase includes practicing your vision, that is, living in the foreshadowing of your vision. It is the transition stage to the realization of the vision. Referencing the vision of Abraham in Genesis 12 NIV, when God unveiled a vision of being a great nation, Abraham did not know what it meant to be a great nation. When he finally got to the Promised Land, I can only imagine his disappointment. The Promised Land that was supposed to be flowing with milk and honey had no evidence of greatness on it. Yet still, the Lord took Abraham to the land of Egypt for him to have a glimpse of what a great nation would look like (Genesis 12:10-20 NKJV). Egypt was probably the greatest nation on earth at that time, so it made perfect sense that he would go there to witness and experience a great nation. God gave Abraham a look into his future and the ability to practice being a great nation. Abraham and Sarah saw a prototype of their future in the land of Egypt. I believe the faith of Abraham and Sarah may have been lifted seeing the glamor, splendor, and the level of services provided to Pharaoh and his officials. Sarah had a first-hand experience when she was taken to Pharaoh's palace. After experiencing the greatness of Egypt, Abraham and Sarah returned to the Promised Land full of confidence and ready to become a great nation. A similar experience of living in the foreshadowing of his vision was presented to David when he was sent to live in King Saul's palace. In the presence of King Saul, David had a first-hand experience of royalty. That was a foreshadowing of his vision of becoming the king of Israel, a position he was anointed for. He left the palace with an authentic experience, which sustained him even during the times of difficulty and uncertainty. I believe reminiscing on his experience in the palace provided sustained encouragement during his tough times in the desert.

Practicing your vision could also mean employing and activating the tasks within your vision. If you want to become a powerful prayer warrior, practice praying long hours by yourself in your prayer closet before that can be translated into long prayer hours publicly. To become a great preacher, practice preaching to yourself privately before you can become a great public preacher. What you have not mastered in private, you cannot display in public. God has opened the door for some of you to work in a corporate organization, not for the purpose of granting you secured jobs, but so that you may experience the nuances of managing an organization effectively and efficiently as a preparation towards starting yours. For some of you, God has brought you in contact with millionaires and billionaires, not for you to serve them, but because that is where He is taking you. He is offering you a glimpse of how to manage great wealth successfully. Some prospective ministers have been brought into contact with great men and women of God for experiencing the nuances of ministry before they are unleashed to establish their vision of ministry. You may have been called to serve a married couple or a family, not because God wants you to be a servant, but for the purpose of you experiencing a family and married life, a recipe of success for your future marriage or family. The opportunity to practice or live through your vision is a sure way of having a real time experience before the manifestation or realization of the vision.

Visionaries ought to be sensitive and detect when they are placed in the position of foreshadow. If God is preparing you for the position of authority, he will send you to the position of servanthood before elevating you through the ranks of authority. Through that, you will practice how to live **under** authority and how to live **with** authority. For he who cannot live under authority cannot live with authority.

The gestational period is the duration of growth of the vision and may include skill development and application, refining the vision, creating a prototype, or living in a foreshadowing. The ability to acquire these essential skills is key for the successful initiation of the next phase.

4. THE REALIZATION/BIRTH PHASE

"Son of man, behold, they of the house of Israel say, the vision that he seeth is for many days to come, and he prophesieth of the times that are far off. Therefore say unto them, Thus saith the Lord God; There shall none of my words be prolonged any more, but the word which I have spoken shall be done, saith the Lord God." Ezekiel 12:27- 28 KJV

The final phase of every vision is the realization, or the phase of manifestation. At this stage, the current and future states have merged into a single unit while the initial gap has been eliminated. Knowledge and skills have been acquired, developed, and applied to enable the vision to be practiced, tried, and tested. Those who witness the vision may now extend their help and talents and become contributors and beneficiaries of the outcome. Though the realization of the vision is the final phase, it must be maintained to ensure its permanence and growth.

Jack Welch, the renowned former CEO of General Electric, is noted to have said, "Good business leaders create a vision, articulate the vision, passionately own the vision, and relentlessly drive it to completion." This indicates that all the preceding phases of a vision are important and must come to completion to become beneficial. Until a vision is brought to completion, the benefits will not be realized. Organizations' visions are realized when they begin to operate and experience the benefits within the vision. Realization of your vision brings fulfillment, reduces or eliminates the burden, and when well executed brings satisfaction.

5. DORMANCY PHASE

Dormancy is a period in the life of the vision where activities or progress may be stalled, suspended, or absent. Some visions may experience a dormant period due to multiple reasons, but not all visions go through this exceptional phase. Therefore, the dormancy phase is an exception and should not be considered as a regular phase of a vision. During the dormant period, no activity takes place, and the vision just lies in waiting. Reasons for dormancy may include the following: need for a vision dependency such as advancement in technology to be fulfilled, mobilization of resources for vision implementation, clarification of the vision, waiting for the right environment before implementation, change in implementation strategy, or re-planning of the implementation path. In certain instances, dormancy may be essential for recalibration and to refocus. However, no matter the purpose, this phase must be managed well to avert potential derailment, premature birth, or abandonment. If your vision is experiencing dormancy, you must still ensure periodic visitation to maintain the desire for its fulfillment. Whatever the issue is, just do not allow your vision to be dormant for too long, since dormancy has the potential of killing the vision entirely. Therefore, it is vital that if your vision goes through this exceptional phase, you apply the necessary checks to limit its duration, continue to manage the vision to maintain your interest, and feed it to keep it alive.

NO	PHASE OF VISION	MAJOR CHARACTERISTICS
1	**CONCEPTION PHASE**	• May recognize and appreciate the problem, challenge, or need. • May harbor a desire to provide solution • May have a promising idea of the potential solution • Presence of a strong, burning desire, uncommon worry, unceasing visualization of the vision, and relentlessness in one's soul. • The vision becomes clear • Sometimes the gap between the current and the future states becomes clear
2	**PREPARATORY PHASE**	• Acquisition, interpretation, and understanding of requisite knowledge • Alternative paths to achieving the vision may be identified • Some potential risks may emerge in this phase • The true gap between the current and the future state is identified.

3	**GESTATIONAL PHASE**	• Development of relevant skills • The right environment must be created and sustained throughout this phase • Potential challenges, risks, and issues may be encountered in this phase • Some visions may be practiced in this phase i.e., some may develop a prototype or live in the foreshadowing of their vision • The gap between the current and future state begins to diminish
4	**REALIZATION PHASE**	• All the components of the vision comes together. • The vision is realized or fully manifested. • People begin to derive benefits from the vision • The gap between the current and future state is closed, i.e., the current state is the same as the future state (the vision) • The stress, burden, and desire experienced in the conception phase are laid to rest
5	**DORMANT PHASE**	• This is an exception phase and not ALL visions may experience dormancy • Activities or progress may be stalled, suspended, or absent • This exception phase may be experienced during preparatory, incubation, or realization phases • Dormancy may be essential in certain cases, such as the need for a dependency to be fulfilled. • Has the potential of aborting the vision

Chapter Summary

Phases of vision: There are four main nonlinear phases of a vision and a fifth exceptional phase.

- Conception Phase: The conception phase is marked by either comprehension of the magnitude of issue, need or problem, a burning desire for change, solution, or transformation. There are two main types of conception, namely, instant and progressive conception.

- Preparatory Phase: The mark for the preparatory phase is acquisition of relevant and the right amount of knowledge.

- Gestational Phase: This is the period of development and refining of applicable skills; sometimes it may include experiencing the vision prototype or living in the foreshadowing. Sometimes the vision is practiced during this phase.

- Realization Phase: This phase is marked by the manifestation or realization of the elements of the vision. This is where the vision comes to fruition and provides benefits to its beneficiaries.

- Dormancy Phase: This is an exceptional phase and may not be present in every vision. The period where activities or progress may be stalled, suspended or absent. Dormancy may occur due to multiple reasons, such as need for a fulfillment of vision dependency, mobilization of resources, clarification of vision, change in implementation strategy, or re-planning implementation strategy.

CHAPTER EIGHT

THE CONSEQUENCES OF LACK OF VISION

("If you don't have a vision, you're going to be stuck in what you know. And the only thing you know is what you've already seen."
– Iyanla Vanzant)

"Where there is no vision, the people perish: but he that keepeth the law, happy is he."
Proverbs 29:18 KJV

VISION STORY- YAHOO INC.

Yahoo Inc. was established by Jerry Yang and David Filo in January 1994 and was one of the pioneers of the early Internet era in the 1990s. Yahoo grew rapidly throughout the 1990s, became a public company in April 1996, and its stock price rose 600% within two years. However, probably due to lack of vision, the company missed opportunities to recognize the potential of companies like Google and Microsoft. In 1998, Google's founders approached Yahoo to sell Google for $1 million, but Yahoo refused. In 2002, Yahoo had the opportunity to buy Google for $1 billion, but executives delayed until Google's price had increased to $3 billion.

In February 2008 and May 2008, Microsoft made an unsolicited bid to acquire Yahoo for $44.6 billion and $47 billion respectively but Yahoo rejected the bid, claiming that it "substantially undervalues" the company and was not in the interest of its shareholders, demanding another 10%+ increase to the offer. Microsoft canceled their offer in May 2008. As of March 2024, Microsoft market capitalization stands at about $3 trillion, Google $1.7 trillion and Yahoo at about $27 billion.

INTRODUCTION

"One of the paramount tragedies of life is not death but absent of vision."

One of the single greatest causes of human failure is lack of vision; the greatest tragedy of humanity is not death but the absence of a vision. Without vision, you live a hopelessly chaotic, fragmented, and disappointed life with no motivation, enthusiasm, or thrust to move forward. You are effortlessly stopped by the presence of a single minuscule obstacle. A nation will rise and fall not based on resource availability but based on vision or lack of it. Lack of vision has caused the disintegration of many marriages and homes, the bankruptcy of many corporations, the shutdown of nations, the abysmal performance of institutions, the stagnation of many professional and ministerial endeavors, and the disappointment of many lives. Many nations abound in resources, but their citizens are languishing in poverty while others who may not have such resources are building and promoting wealth among its citizens; all because there is no vision. You can have the best education, resources, position, profession, wife, husband, children, and opportunity but without vision, they will amount to nothing. Lack of vision has caused many to take their talents, skills, innovations, ideas, and potential into the grave. Without vision, your opportunities will be seen as burdens, your springboards as obstacles, friends as enemies, helpers as challengers, partners as competitors. and the likes.

Let us look at a tale of two countries below:

Singapore is about 275 square miles (smaller than the state of Rhode Island), and is inhabited by five million people. The country gained independence from Britain on August 9, 1965. It has almost no natural resources, but in 2021, their per capita GDP was 72,794.00 USD.

In contrast, Ghana is 92,101 square miles, with an estimated population of about 33 million as of 2022. The country can boast of an almost unlimited supply of gold, diamonds, timber, oil, and other natural resources. However, Ghana has a per capita GDP of $2,353.

The significant success achieved by Singapore, a country with literally no natural resources, is because of the vision of their late leader Lee Yew. President Lee's vision of making Singapore a financial hub of Asia and the world positioned the tiny, resourceless Singapore as one of the greatest success stories in modern day economic development. A person, society, nation, or people of no vision can at best be ordinary and at worst live in abject failure.

THE TWO STRONGHOLDS OF BEING VISIONLESS

Nothing just happens; there is a cause or reason for everything that happens in this world. People with no vision have reasons for their non-achievement. Through my interaction with many people across the globe and from diverse backgrounds, I have identified two main strongholds of a visionless person, which I term the **Tower of Blame** and **the Road of Excuses**. Whenever you engage a visionless person in any conversation, you are sure to encounter either or both of the strongholds identified above.

The Tower of Blame: A visionless person easily takes refuge in the tower of blame. Examples include the visionless student blaming the professor for a failing grade, an athlete blaming the coach for his or her inabilities, a spouse or child blaming the other for the disintegration of their relationship, and the government or citizen blaming the other for the community/society's downfall. The list is just endless. However, meet a visionary and you will see that blame is not part of their vocabulary. Visionless people are unable to take responsibility for their actions.

I once met a young African woman during one of my counseling sessions who was passionately blaming her parents for "Bringing her to a university in America and abandoning her." During my counseling session, I realized that her parents had brought her to a good university in the United States, supported her financially, and provided for her well-being. Because of lack of vision, she consistently maintained a low grade point average (GPA), until she missed the opportunity of graduating with her bachelor's degree. I informed the young lady that there were millions of young people in the world aspiring to have a fraction of the opportunity she has in life. She was just visionless and resorted to blaming everybody including her parents who have probably sacrificed significantly to bring her to a university in the United States.

The Road of Excuses: The other stronghold for the visionless is what I term the Road of Excuses. It is much easier to travel on the road of excuses than to find reasons to pursue a vision. Such people have mastered the art of finding excuses for their failures. They easily take refuge in well-crafted excuses and sometimes may rationalize their own excuses. Those who are serious in pursuing a vision, goal, or objective will find a way, not an excuse. Many do not understand that excuses only make today easier but tomorrow harder, while discipline makes today harder but tomorrow easier. Excuses manifest in the form of pretense or subterfuge, which sometimes can logically or easily be overcome. The road of excuses is easy to travel on since it requires minimal effort, but it leads only to the city of failure.

On the political front, I have realized that a conversation with most African leaders on the plight of their people ends in either hearing some kind of blame or some flimsy excuse. Many of our leaders do not have the willpower to own their failures, accept their responsibilities, and embrace challenges for positive change. Remember, it is easier to find an excuse and push the blame on someone than to create a solution. Some blame colonial masters, opposing political parties, institutions, resources, citizens, and anything they can easily push the blame onto. The irony is that most of these countries have achieved political independence for decades but are still blaming colonial masters.

One positive way to set yourself free from these strongholds is to determine in your heart never to blame anyone for your plight or find an excuse for your current condition. Replace blame with responsibility. Take responsibility for your actions and consequences; this increases self-awareness, confidence, and self-esteem. Develop a mindset that as far as your life is concerned, the onus of success or failures will always lie on you. Remember that, though you cannot change your past, you can always influence your future. Blame no one for your past failures and give no excuse to that effect, either. Take full responsibility for your life, irrespective of your experiences. Yes, granted, parents may not have provided the right opportunities, that boss may have treated you very badly, that spouse may have taken undue advantage of you, that man of God may have acted non-Christlike, that friend may have said something really bad or disappointed you, but as long as you maintain your focus on the vision, all these obstacles can be turned into springboards to propel you forward. Every experience of failure was meant to prepare you for your future success. Permit no excuse to derail you from the path to your vision. If you exit from the road of excuses and come out from your tower of blame, you will find a reason to remain on the path to your destiny.

SIX CONSEQUENCES OF LACK OF VISION

1. LACK OF DIRECTION

It is said that every road leads to your destiny if you do not know where you are going. Human beings function at their absolute best when they are working towards accomplishing something that is important to them. Successful people have a clear sense of direction and what they want to accomplish in life. Life is a journey, with start and end points. Every human being was created for a purpose. Unfortunately, most people never stop to consider or try to discover their real purpose in life. When you look at unsuccessful people or those who seem to be unhappy in their lives, you can absolutely bet that they have a limited or no sense of direction. The journey of life is intertwined, with many crisscrossing each other's path. The end state of one's journey is the beginning of another's. Those who follow others' paths are likely to miss their destination. Those who have limited or no sense of direction easily drift to follow others. Without clear-cut vision, there will be limited or no sense of direction.

It is estimated that the journey between Egypt and Canaan could be undertaken within days. A distance that should have taken a few days to complete took about 40 years for the Israelites. The difference in time between what could have been and what really happened is just beyond reasoning. When people lack a sense of direction, a journey that should last them a few days may take many years. The degree, career, family, project, ministry, business, children may take a ridiculously longer time to bring to the point of success due to lack of direction. The reason is that on the journey to your destiny, you may encounter troubles, temptations, obstacles, challenges, difficulties, and hurdles. These hurdles may present an opportunity if you do not seek an alternative or shortcut. In the midst of all the above, the vision serves as the North Star to direct your life. Therefore, without a vision, you will have no sense of direction.

2. LACK OF DESTINATION

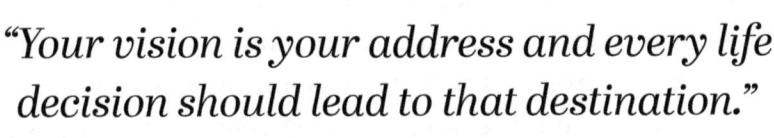

"Your vision is your address and every life decision should lead to that destination."

Every journey must have a destination, which is the realization of vision. Your vision is your address, and every life decision must lead to that address. A destination is a place of rest; therefore, a life without destiny is characterized by restlessness. The lack of vision implies no visible point of achievement or rest. God's vision of creation ended with the making of humanity, after which God rested (Genesis 2:1-2). The visionless person has no point of achievement, settlement, or rest. In the leadership vision created by Jethro (read Jethro-Moses leadership vision: Exodus 18), Jethro identified a four-point milestone manifestation as the signs of the attainment of the vision. Upon achievement of the vision, Moses would be less exhausted due to delegating responsibilities to God-fearing and trustworthy judges and the people would no longer have to queue all day and would go home satisfied. When your vision is clear, time-bound, measurable, and solution-bound, achievement of these milestones indicate attainment of the vision. Some people are confused in life because they do not know where they are going or what they are working towards. This is partly the hidden reason for the development of hostility, drug addiction, alcoholism, violence, depression, and many psychosomatic illnesses.

A visionless person has no futuristic state of reference, no means of assessment and evaluation of progress. Assessment and evaluation of progress are vital in generating hope for living. Without vision, progress cannot be assessed, and hope may be elusive. So therefore, visionlessness breeds hopelessness.

Today I want to encourage you to set up a well-defined, attainable vision for your life. Usually, I encourage people to establish a vision for their overall life as well as area-specific visions. Prospective couples should set an unclouded vision for their marriage and family life. Young professionals are to define the periscope of their vision for career success to avoid ambiguity in their career. Aspiring ministers are to wait on God for their ministerial vision before commencing any ministerial journey. This will help alleviate ministerial copycating and its associated inefficiencies that are becoming so prevalent in Christendom. Against the backdrop of your vision, try to have clarity of at least the next step to the destination to help you realize it upon attainment; remember, those who have no vision have no destination.

3. LACK OF DISCIPLINE

A disciplined life revolves around honesty, hard work, self-motivation, encouragement, living within a set of rules and regulations and focusing on executing tasks. A disciplined life ensures stability, responsibility, and provides people the opportunity of living efficiently and effectively. Vision is an enforcing agent of discipline.

Lack of discipline may manifest through waste of resources and is present in a visionless life. A disciplined life is important for the utilization of limited resources like time. Therefore, disciplined individuals accomplish more within the 24 hours available to everyone than undisciplined people. For many individuals, an undisciplined life is an indication of lack of vision. Meet an undisciplined husband and you will find a visionless man. Visit the home of an undisciplined wife and you are under the roof of a visionless woman. Work with an undisciplined boss and a visionless superior is managing you. Live in an undisciplined society or community and you are living among visionless people. Where there is vision, there is discipline, and the lack thereof is the cause of restlessness, lawlessness, and chaotic lifestyles and societies. Remember, your vision will discipline you for the purpose of its achievement.

4. LACK OF LEADERSHIP

Lack of leadership refers to leaders' inability to lead, direct and/or exert influence over their followers. True leadership is not about position but rather about action and interaction. You are not a leader because of the position you occupy or the title before your name; you are a leader by your decisions and actions. Decisions and actions are the defining values of leadership, the ability to influence without coercion or force. True leadership influence is executed in such a subtle manner that those who are being influenced are oblivious to it. Having unclouded vision and setting goals are the hallmark of true leaders. Lack of leadership is the inability to influence and set directions; this is often due to lack of vision and goals. Lack of leadership is one of the greatest crises in the world today; people are occupying positions without vision and providing no leadership.

Examples of visionless leaders are present all over the world. Sometimes you will be stunned upon commencing a conversation about their vision with people in leadership positions. From the store manager to the school president, from the CEO to the politician, from the minister to the church leader, some leaders have absolutely no or faint vision for their position or organization. Therefore, many of these so-called leaders are occupying positions with no commensurate development or any transformative agenda. Work is a mechanical routine, as many have memorized their studies to graduation and are still memorizing their work to stagnation. There is no vision to challenge the status quo.

A friend of mine shared his experience with me, which highlights this sentiment of lack of vision among many leaders. He stated that several years after graduating from high school, he decided to visit his alma mater in an attempt to contribute towards the development of the school. Unfortunately, within minutes of conversing with the school principal, he realized the man had no vision for the school. Instead of trying to transform the school, he blamed his predecessor for an uncompleted school building, some teachers for their lack of commitment to their profession, students for not exhibiting seriousness towards their education, and the list went on. My friend politely asked the principal why he was hired and brought to the school. The principal's answer was an addition of blaming and rationalization of his excuses, confirming the initial assessment of my friend. I share this story not to look down on anyone, but to highlight the fact that every leader must come to terms with the importance of having a vision. God does not place people in positions of authority just for titles and occupancy's sake, but to enable the execution of vision and exert positive influence. Ask yourself these questions: why am I here? What is the purpose of the title bestowed upon me? What benefits are people going to derive from the way I fill my position? A reflection on the questions above will set the tone for discovery of purpose and facilitate the formation of vision.

True leadership is about vision development and execution. If we are to bring about the needed transformation in our societies, we must have visionary leaders. Our politicians, teachers, CEO, managers, workers, parents, students, market women, ministers, pastors, church members, civil servants, and the like must have and pursue a vision for their positions. The lack of vision is the cause of many leadership failures. Every leader must have a vision to guide their decisions and direct them towards their intended destiny.

5. LACK OF INSPIRATION/MOTIVATION

People are motivated when they know what they are doing is worthy and may lead them to a desired end. A well-defined vision can bring clarity to your sense of direction, purpose, and destiny. Vision can motivate you by providing a visualization of a future state that inspires you to perform the necessary actions needed for its attainment. It gives you something to look forward to and work towards. Some people are motivated by the passion their vision generates. The vision generates passion, inspiration, and compelling desire, which drives the bearer towards the end state. It is like a string that pulls you, and once you are being pulled toward your bigger future, motivation comes on its own.

Lack of vision therefore creates a vacuum of inspiration, absence of fervent desire, and unwillingness to gather yourself for attainment of your purpose. If you lack motivation, check your vision. Either the vision is not clear enough, not well understood, or not time- bound. There are those who may have vision all right, but when it is not time-bound, that vision provides no impetus or desire towards its fulfillment. The lack of time-bound vision may take away any sense of urgency. When your vision is well conceived, pondered over, and ubiquitous in your life, you are inspired to overcome every challenge and obstacle on your path.

6. LACK OF PURPOSE

"Purpose is the original intent for creation and the reason for existence."

Many tragedies exist on this earth, but a life without purpose surpasses them all. Purpose is the original intent for creation and the reason for existence. The intent of creation, innovation, manufacturing of anything defines its purposes. Therefore, the source of existence is the ideal place for purpose discovery. The one who created you or brought you into existence has a purpose for your life. The barometer to measure true success is against the fulfillment of one's purpose. If you are working towards your life's purpose, then you are on your path to success. However, there is no purpose without vision; your vision will inform your purpose. If you do not know the reason for your existence, you have no sense of direction, priorities, reason for accomplishment, or vision and your usefulness is in doubt. Understanding your purpose establishes the right environment for the conception, development, growth, and realization of your vision.

We live in a world of competing alternatives; every day we are bombarded with multiple options and faced with the opportunity of making choices. To make the right choice, you must first identify your options, prioritize, and choose the ones that will take you to achieving your goals, visions, and purpose. Prioritization helps us to manage our time and energy efficiently, gives a sense of focus, and prevents us from being busy with everything but achieving little or nothing. Working towards a set vision will help you with setting priorities and making choices that will lead to the realization of the vision. Good alternatives that may not lead to vision realization are left behind.

CONCLUSION

Always remember that in order to avoid the consequences of lack of vision, tie your vision to your purpose; one cannot survive without the other. Purposeless and visionless people live aimlessly frustrated with no sense of discipline and no measure of success and accomplishment. As the Bible says in Proverbs 29:18 KJV, "where there is no vision, the people perish, but he that keepeth the law, happy is he." It is extremely important that the force of vision drives individuals, institutions, organizations, and nations. Lack of vision produces lack of direction, destination, discipline, leadership, inspiration, and purpose.

Chapter Summary

- Lack of Vision: Lack of vision is one of the single greatest failures of humanity and the greatest tragedy is the absence of vision, not death. It has impacted every dimension of humanity including marriage, career, education, ministry, politics, institution, corporate organizations, communities, and nations.

- Excuses and Blame: Visionless individuals easily resort to excuses and blame to justify their actions and inactions in life. Excuses are means of justifying one's actions and inaction while blame shifts responsibility to others.

- The following are six consequences of lack of vision:

  - Lack of Direction: Successful people have a clear sense of direction in life. Lack of vision implies no sense of direction, and this is manifested as an unorganized, haphazard road that leads to nowhere.

  - Lack of Destination: Your vision is your address; where there is no vision there is no destination. Lack of vision implies no visible point of achievement or rest.

  - Lack of Discipline: A disciplined life ensures stability and responsibility and provides people the opportunity of living efficiently and effectively. Vision is an enforcing agent of discipline, and the lack of vision removes restraint.

  - Lack of Leadership: Leadership is about influence. Where there is no vision, there is no force of influence and impetus of encouragement for achievement.

THE CONSEQUENCES OF LACK OF VISION

- Lack of Inspiration and Motivation: Vision generates an intrinsic fuel that propels an individual or organization through the channel of progress. This is manifested as an inspiration that provides hope and expectation towards its realization. The intrinsic energy also generates the thrust to overcome obstacles and challenges.

- Lack of Purpose: Purpose is the original intent for creation and the reason for existence. Where there is no vision, purpose is compromised or unidentified. An existence without vision lacks reason for survival and is prone to perish.

CHAPTER NINE

FORMS OF VISION

("Create the highest, grandest vision possible for your life, because you become what you believe." – Oprah Winfrey)

"The vision concerning Judah and Jerusalem that Isaiah son of Amoz saw during the reigns of Uzziah, Jotham, Ahaz and Hezekiah, kings of Judah."
Isaiah 1:1 NIV

VISION STORY- KWAME NKRUMAH

At the onset of the twentieth century, the gloom of European colonization hovered over the continent of Africa. This dark cloud was to be expelled by the birth of a visionary, Dr. Kwame Nkrumah of Ghana. His vision to restore the dignity of the African lost through slavery and colonialism and to enable the African to function freely in the coming world society as an equal player and partner was no easy task. However, this vision generated an unquenchable internal desire to champion an anti-colonialism movement globally that resulted in the political freedom (at least on paper) for many African countries. Nkrumah's midnight speech and his declaration that "Our independence is meaningless unless it is linked up with total liberation of the African continent" on declaring Ghana's independence was a trailblazing revolutionary rhetoric that ignited the wildfire against colonial chains. Over the next few decades since the political independence of Ghana, leaders of multiple African countries would mount different political platforms to make similar proclamations to its citizens. Today, Dr. Kwame Nkrumah's vision is seen as a model of African political leadership capable of liberating the continent from Western Imperialism.

INTRODUCTION

There are two main forms of vision, namely, individual/personal and corporate/institutional vision. The forms of vision are categorized based on the primary entity or object of impact upon the realization of the vision. If the primary object of impact is a person, such vision is categorized as an individual vision. On the other hand, if the primary object of impact is a group of people, such vision is termed a corporate vision.

Individual/Personal Vision

This category of vision is meant to bring into reality the future state of an individual, but may happen through the involvement of other people. God called Abraham and gave him a vision that depicted his future state. This vision was specifically for Abraham, although it would later translate to inform the future state of the nation Israel. Mostly, a well-executed individual vision would need the involvement of other people and would be beneficial to others. Jesus' vision was to establish the Kingdom of God on earth, but that required the involvement of the Apostles, prophets, evangelists, pastors, teachers, and other workers (Ephesians 4:11-12 NKJV).

Corporate Vision

The second category of vision is the corporate (organizational or institutional) vision. This form of vision is usually conceived by an individual but for the purpose of an organization or institution. It brings into reality the future state of an organization and therefore its implementation requires the acceptance and involvement of members of such organization. Corporate vision may apply to small institutions with few members, a global conglomerate with millions of employees, or nations of diverse numbers of citizens. Though an individual or a few people usually conceive it, such a vision will need to cascade throughout the organization over time. This is because, in most cases, members may join an organization with different visions. The differences in their various visions may begin to evaporate and merge into a common one through the cascading effect.

Most corporate and well-established institutions have a well-written and articulated vision that guides the decision and direction of the whole organization towards a common goal. Some nations also have national growth and development visions, which is well understood and appreciated by its citizenry and guides the enactment of laws, policies, and the overall operations of the nation. In such cases, the national vision is held in high esteem and continues to serve as the driving force behind every decision even under multiparty democratic systems.

Just as individuals, organizations, and nations have their visions, God also had a vision when He created the universe. In Habakkuk 2:2-3, the Prophet Habakkuk was encouraged to write down a vision he saw because it was for an appointed time. God has a master vision to establish and build His Kingdom (Matthew 16:18 NKJV) that will prevail over the gates of Hades, possess nations and humanity, and subject the universe under His rulership.

However, no individual denomination can execute the totality of God's vision. God has therefore given some part of His vision as plans to certain denominations, churches, or para-church organizations.

Every church or denomination has an area of focus within the master vision of God. Every denomination is implementing part of God's master plan. Therefore, it is incumbent on church leaders to embark on extensive prayers to unveil the vision and work toward its realization. Lotich affirms, "All the churches working together participate in weaving the tapestry of God's perfect plan around the world." (Lotich, 2020) By this logic, though all churches may be reading the same Bible, they may have different areas of focus as inspired by the Holy Spirit to bring the master plan to fruition.

Organizational leaders must know the reason for the existence of their institution, assess its current and future states, and devise appropriate transitional strategies needed to attain the future state. "This is why it is essential to have a guiding mission, vision, and value statement that articulates why the organization exists, where it proposes to go, and what guiding principles will help direct its decision-making." (Lotich, 2020) Vision helps to set a clear path into the future and provides guidance even during turbulent times or cloudy weather. A well-guided institution can maintain its course and avoid potentially drifting in an alternative direction or uncharted territory. A vision statement serves the purpose of guiding the organization. Jesus' vision is for the world to be saved through Him (John 3:17). This vision was revealed to the Apostle Paul in 1 Timothy 2:4. A saved world and humanity is the vision of our Lord and Savior Jesus Christ.

THE VISION STATEMENT

In our reference Scripture above, the Lord told the Prophet Habakkuk to write the vision down. Writing the vision down is an inherent and urgent call to leaders who desire to establish a path of continuity for their organizations. It is a tool and a document that helps the organization to achieve its goal and intended purpose. A well-crafted, communicated, and understood vision not only ensures that members are aware of the intended goal but also helps to solicit their interest and amass membership support for implementation. Some companies have assumed a reactive approach toward the development of their vision; however, a careful study of Scripture should inspire every leader to proactively create a transformative, goal-oriented, solution-based environment capable of producing visionary leaders who are poised to influence the world with Biblical values and principles.

A vision statement is usually two or three sentences that espouse the organizational goal or its intended future state. However, I have realized over time that writing a few high-level vision sentences leaves room for speculation, assumptions, and diverse interpretation (and misinterpretation). To avoid all these potential triggers of derailment, every organization or individual is encouraged to produce and be guided by a well-thought-out vision plan.

Let us look at the following processes for writing a good vision document.

Identification and Definition of Vision

Identifying and defining the vision is the first step toward establishing a successful goal-oriented structure. It answers the question, WHAT? What is your institution/individual aspiring to achieve in the end? What is the perceived ideal future state of the organization?

Below are some questions that may guide the writing of a vision statement:

- What ultimate impact do we want our organization/individual to achieve?

- How do we see the future of our organization in the short, medium, and long term?

- What will be its future state? What will have changed?

- What legacy do we want to leave in our marketplace through our organization?

- How will our vision inspire, motivate, and encourage our team or our community?

Answering these questions will set the tone for writing the vision statement.

Writing the vision down ensures its preservation (sometimes for an appointed time), accessibility, and understandability, and provides the opportunity for accurate interpretation. A good vision statement/document must have these five characteristics; clarity, time-bound, solution-bound, achievable, and measurable.

VISION AND MISSION

An organization uses vision statements to express their future aspirations, while using mission statements to present their purpose. Both statements may assist organizations in prioritizing their goals and are driving forces in the decision making process.

A good vision and mission statement ought to be clear, concise, memorable, achievable, and understandable. Jesus knew His mission, which was "I have come that they may have life, and have it to the full." John 10:10b NIV It is important for every prospective leader to identify and know their mission before embarking on any leadership journey.

The life of Jesus Christ was mission-oriented in every form and dimension. Even at an early age, Jesus focused on going about the Father's business. His mission to seek and save lost souls (Luke 19:10 NIV) was enshrined in everything He did throughout His earthly ministry and must inform the mission of every church. His mission to save lost souls inspired the great commission (Matthew 28:16-20 NKJV), a call to save the world and raise people with Christ-like character. Church procedures, principles, values, and systems must all rest on establishing and promoting soul-winning, teaching, and building souls into maturity.

The mission statement of The Church of Pentecost is stated as: "We exist to establish responsible and self-sustaining churches filled with committed, Spirit-filled Christians of character, who will impact their communities." (https://thecophq.org/mission-vision/)

The Church of Pentecost USA Inc. states its mission with a different spin. "The Church exists to bring all people everywhere to the saving knowledge of our Lord Jesus Christ through the proclamation of the gospel, the planting of churches and the equipping of believers for every God-glorifying service. It demonstrates the love of God through the provision of social services in partnership with governments, communities, and other like-minded organizations."

Another example of a Christ-centered mission statement is that of Grace Community Church in Marietta, Georgia. Their mission "is to spread the good news of Jesus to all people by **Encouraging** the saved, **Equipping** the saints, and **Evangelizing** the lost," which is summarized as the 3Es, Encourage, Equip and Evangelize." It is imperative that every church's mission reflects Jesus' mission and revolves around the great commission in order to maintain and align with the purpose of God.

Chapter Summary

- Forms of Vision: Describes the channel of its manifestation and the magnitude of its primary impact upon realization.

- Individual Vision: Is a form of vision with a primary purpose of impacting an individual upon its realization.

- Corporate Vision: Is a form of vision with a primary purpose of impacting an organization or an institution upon its realization.

- Vision Statement: Is a tool and a document that helps an organization or individual to achieve their vision, goal, or intended purpose.

- Vision and Mission: Whereas a vision is a description of the future state of an individual or an organization, a mission is a description of the purpose or reason of existence for an individual or an organization.

CHAPTER TEN

VISION CASTING AND MAPPING

("The vision of a champion is bent over, drenched in sweat, at the point of exhaustion when nobody else is looking." – Mia Hamm)

> *"And the LORD answered me, and said, Write the vision, and make it plain upon tables, that he may run that readeth it."*
>
> **Habakkuk 2:2 (KJV)**

VISION STORY- OPRAH WINFREY

Oprah Winfrey is a billionaire media mogul, philanthropist, Emmy Award-winning talk show host, Academy Award-nominated actress, cultural icon, Television Academy Hall of Famer, a former Miss Black Tennessee, the world's first Black woman billionaire in 2003, who has broken barriers and shattered every form of ceiling. Best known for hosting her internationally popular talk show *The Oprah Winfrey Show* from 1986 to 2011. Winfrey has used her platform to empower, inspire, and advocate for positive change. Her philanthropic efforts, particularly in education and healthcare, showcase a commitment to making a lasting impact beyond the business world.

Oprah Gail Winfrey was born on January 29, 1954, in the rural town of Kosciusko, Mississippi. Her Aunt Ida named her after the biblical figure Orpah, but due to difficulty in pronunciation, her family began spelling it Oprah. Her early childhood was marked by family difficulty including multiple forms of abuse. Winfrey's vision of becoming a talk show host was challenged by racism, sexism, and all the forms of discrimination that were prevalent at the time. However, she did not allow any of those challenges and obstacles to prevent her from pursuing her vision, and in 1986, she launched *The Oprah Winfrey Show*, becoming the first Black female host of a nationally syndicated daily talk show. With its placement on 120 channels and an audience of 10 million people, the show grossed $125 million by the end of its first year. Indeed, she had said, "My idea is to give hope, because where there is no hope, there is no vision, and where there is no vision, people will perish."

INTRODUCTION

"Vision casting is a term used in leadership and strategic planning that refers to creating a compelling, inspiring vision and communicating it for an organization or team. This vision provides the group with a clear direction and purpose and serves as a roadmap for achieving long-term goals and objectives. The act of vision casting involves communicating the vision to all members of the organization or team to ensure that everyone is aligned and working towards the same goal. This may be achieved through various methods, such as team meetings, presentations, and use of visual aids. The goal of vision casting is to create a shared sense of purpose and direction among team members, which can lead to increased motivation, productivity, and success.

"Vision casting is a valuable tool for leaders and visionaries to map out the future of their organization. It includes setting a vision, creating actionable steps to achieve it, and regularly evaluating progress. Vision casting combines strategy and vision in an intuitive package that allows stakeholders to execute the plan easily. Through vision casting, people can prepare for uncertainty by forecasting potential risks, taking ownership of the vision, and becoming inspired as they witness it unfolding. Various software solutions for vision casting allow customized plans, comprehensive control over strategy execution processes, and smarter decision-making. It is all about crafting a vision you believe in, taking responsibility for it, and building a winning team around it!" (https://www.rhythmsystems.com/blog/vision-casting-a-leaders-job)

No matter how powerful a vision may be conceived, without it being casted properly, it will continue to be a dream. Although vision casting may be time consuming, its importance and impact on the team outweighs any amount of time invested in it.

"Transformative leaders are visionary leaders."

History has taught us that transformational leaders are visionary leaders. Globalization, availability of social media, and emergence of international organizations (including churches) have unearthed new dimensions of organizational challenges. These dimensions require strong visionaries with in-depth understanding of administration along with a solid multinational view of management to be at the helm of affairs. With this new, challenging environment, customers are gradually shifting from loyalty to one product or service to a need-based orientation. This diminishing character of loyalty is even affecting faith-based organizations. Under this system, the focus is more on meeting an immediate need. Believers solicit the Word of God, prayers, and other spiritual needs from multiple sources. Therefore, sharing vision and amassing membership support is particularly important to restoring a sense of loyalty to products, services, and brands.

VISION MAPPING

Vision mapping is a process used to create a vision map either for an individual or for an organization. The map illustrates the gaps between complex future states (the vision) and current environments, and the plans, projects, and proposals needed to bridge that gap on a single sheet of paper. Vision casting focuses on identifying and unearthing the detailed vision, sharing and amassing support for implementation. On the other hand, vision mapping involves identifying the vision, the current state and the possible steps/activities that need to be taken towards its achievement. In addition, through vision mapping, potential risks may be identified and analyzed; one of the main outputs of vision mapping is a risk register log. This log helps you to determine where and when to deploy caution throughout the implementation process.

Jesus Christ posed a question in Luke 14:28-30 NKJV, "Which one of you wants to embark on a project and does not first assess the cost and availability of funds to determine his ability to complete the project before commencing?" Though the question above is related to cost analysis, it may also be extended to cover a holistic risk analysis. Identifying and analyzing the potential risk in every vision is essential to creating the right navigation through the uncertain terrain and helps to discover the appropriate path to success. The following process may be used to achieve a vision map.

1. IDENTIFY YOUR VISION

Think about your vision, whether personal or corporate. This should commence with a future state in mind. How do you see yourself in a defined future time? Identify all the potential future states that you wish to achieve. Focus on the future self for personal vision or future state for a corporate vision. Prioritize all the identified visions. This exercise can be very scary and intimidating, especially where the reality of the vision seems unrealistic.

2. DOCUMENT YOUR CURRENT STATE

Be honest with yourself and document your current state. This is not what you want to be but what you are currently. This process can also encompass an individual or corporate vision. It can be extremely uncomfortable, particularly where the gap between the current and future states seems unbridgeable. If you feel uncomfortable, it means you have started on a good note. This is the time for your reality check. The journey is not going to be easy, but it is doable, possible, and attainable.

3. IDENTIFY AND MAP OUT YOUR PATHWAYS

The third step is to systematically identify and map out all the possible pathways between the current and future states. There could be multiple pathways to where you want to be and that is okay. Identify as many as you can. The most important thing is making sure that each pathway contains specific steps to help you move closer to your vision. Be careful to highlight potential obstacles, challenges, and risks you may encounter along the way. Properly highlighting these potential objects of derailment will help you take the necessary steps to prepare yourself to overcome them successfully.

Mapping out your pathways should also include the key stakeholders who may influence the success of your journey. Some key stakeholders for individual visions may include family members and friends. On the other hand, corporate stakeholders may include employees, partners, competitors, governments, and investors. For spiritual visions, God is always the number one key stakeholder, because He is the owner of the vision and only uses human beings as vessels to accomplish His purpose. This is why implementation of spiritual vision calls for continuous dependence on God.

4. ANALYZE AND PRIORITIZE YOUR PATHWAYS

The vision map serves as a visual aid to help you visualize each different pathway toward your vision. The ability to take a closer look at each individual activity and challenge along each different pathway will help you make more informed decisions about your life or that of the organization. Having a clear view of each path will help you understand the various possible pathways, help you prioritize, and make the best decision towards its attainment. The idea is to choose the path of optimal experience and outcome and not the path of least resistance. Choosing the path of optimal outcome could mean stepping out of your comfort zone and taking some challenges head on. The path of least resistance may not always produce the desired results. If you truly want to achieve your vision, do not shy away from confronting challenges, facing and overcoming obstacles, and engaging in strategies to mitigate possible risks. A calculated risk- taking could be the right recipe for success.

5. PURSUE YOUR VISION

Keep your vision map in a convenient place and take the first step. Taking the first step could be as minor an event as making a phone call, completing an application, registering a business, buying a bag of cement or a piece of land, or resigning from your current place of employment. In pursuing your vision, focus on the possibility of achieving the next step and not the accomplishment of the vision in total. Consult your vision map frequently, as it serves as a guide to direct your path. Sometimes, the environment may change, which may call for recalibration or updating the map to make it relevant to the present environment. For example, losing the support of a key stakeholder, change in the source or amount of funding, updated governmental policies, withdrawal of an investor, relocation, modification to family composition, and other critical events may call for revision of vision and subsequent update to the vision map. Always remember that the vision map is a plan. It must be flexible enough to accept new opportunities and rigid enough to help you maintain your focus. Periodically updating and revising the vision map is essential to ensure that the map is not just a document but is relevant in guiding you to your destination.

Chapter Summary

- Vision Casting: Is the process of creating a compelling and inspiring vision and communicating it for an organization or team. It is a valuable tool for leaders and visionaries to map out the future or their organization.

- Vision Mapping: Is the process used to create a vision map either for an individual or organization. The vision map illustrates the gap between the complex future state and the current environment, the plans, projects, and proposals needed to bridge that gap. The following are the five main steps for creating a vision map

    - Identify Your Vision (Future State)

    - Document Your Current State

    - Identify and Map out Your Pathways

    - Analyze and Prioritize Your Pathways

    - Pursue Your Vision

(PART TWO PRACTICAL LESSONS
FROM BIBLICAL VISIONS)

CHAPTER ELEVEN

INTRODUCTION TO BIBLICAL/SPIRITUAL VISIONS

("Without the vision of a goal, a man cannot manage his own life, much less the lives of others." - Jack Weatherford)

"While I, Daniel, was watching the vision and trying to understand it, there before me stood one who looked like a man."

Daniel 8:15 NIV

VISION STORY-DAVID YONGGI CHO

David Yonggi Cho was born on February 14, 1936, in a small town in Wooljoo County in South Korea. He started the Yoido Full Gospel Church (YFGC) with only five members on May 18, 1958. However, through a series of spiritual encounters, he conceived a vision of building the world's largest church. Cho resorted to preaching in a loud voice as if he was ministering to a large congregation even when his church members were few, a situation that resulted in his mother-in-law, a close ministerial associate, asking him to speak softly. Cho is recorded saying, "I said, 'Mother, the people I am speaking to are in the canvas of my heart.' In my vision and dream, I have 10,000 people in my church. So, I speak to that 10,000 people." In 1993, with 700,000 members, the Yoido Full Gospel Church was the world's largest Pentecostal Charismatic congregation recognized by the *Guinness Book of World Records*.

INTRODUCTION

We learned earlier that vision is a pictorial or descriptive representation of a future state. One of the greatest gifts God has given humanity is the gift of vision, which is a function of unlimited imagination within the subconscious mind or an unveiling of a spiritual reality. Vision can be realized by spiritual and non-spiritual individuals; in fact, some of the greatest visions ever conceived and birthed have been through non-Christians. Throughout scripture, God showed His vision to those who were called, but rarely unveiled the path towards that vision. He does this to create an opportunity for the visionary to seek His direction and dependence. Seeking God's face and understanding that depending on Him is the only way to fulfill the vision forces character development, provision gathering, and every intrinsic capability needed to achieve and maintain the vision.

In this chapter, we shall review some Biblical visions and determine how they apply to our daily lives. The Bible is full of remarkable visions, with people who saw their future states from their humble background and worked towards its realization. These model stories present great opportunities for our emulation, application, and subsequent attainment of similar feats. The strategies, guidelines, roles, and recommendations in these stories are equally relevant and applicable in our time and are guaranteed to produce similar results when applied faithfully.

Anyone aspiring to achieve greatness can reliably utilize the values and lessons from the story of Abraham. Those seeking to implement excellent leadership strategies may depend on Jethro's recommendations to Moses. Any vision of success has its modalities well spelt out, n the story of Nehemiah, an ideal case for adoption with a guaranteed successful outcome. The story of Joseph presents an enviable administrative lesson for our studies. Inherent in the account of King Solomon are great strategies for kingdom or nation establishment. These strategies, when well adopted and implemented, can easily transition every nation or society into an impeccable level of advancement. The vision of equipping and instituting a dependable plan of succession is unveiled through the ministry of Jesus Christ. The following chapters have a detailed analysis of each of the aforementioned visions and present their remarkable lessons for our adoption.

Chapter Summary

- Definition of Biblical Vision: This is an introduction to a series of Biblical visions that are going to be treated in the subsequent chapters.

CHAPTER TWELVE

THE VISION OF GREATNESS (THE ABRAHAMIC VISION)

("VISION WITHOUT EXECUTION IS DELUSION."
- Thomas A. Edison)

"Now the Lord had said to Abram: 'Get out of your country, From your family And from your father's house, To a land that I will show you. I will make you a great nation; I will bless you And make your name great; And you shall be a blessing. I will bless those who bless you, And I will curse him who curses you; And in you all the families of the earth shall be blessed'."

Genesis 12:1-3 NKJV

"After these thigs the word of the Lord came to Abram in a vision, saying, 'Do not be afraid, Abram. I am your shield, your exceedingly great reward.'"

Genesis 15:1 (NKJV)

VISION STORY- REVEREND JAMES MCKEOWN

Rev. James McKeown was born on September 12th, 1900, in Ballymena, Northern Ireland to Irish parents, William John McKeown and Elizabeth Thompson. He was the first Pentecostal missionary to come to the then Gold Coast (now Ghana) on March 4th 1937, with his wife Sophia McKeown from the United Kingdom and were instrumental in the establishment of The Apostolic Church - Ghana. In the 1950s, they founded the Church of Pentecost after he fell out with the native church leaders for seeking conventional medical treatment instead of spiritual healing. Through multiple prophecies, the Lord declared His covenant of greatness with The Church of Pentecost, which had started in a small village in West Africa. The Lord declared that He would take the church to the ends of the earth; this was practically inconceivable at the time. Today, the Church of Pentecost with its small beginning has spread throughout the world with footprints in about 170 countries and counting. Indeed, every great vision has a small beginning, and therefore do not despise the little things (Zachariah 4:10 NIV).

INTRODUCTION

There is a common saying that vision can see the mountaintop even if the clouds hide it from view. Abram's descriptive vision is well articulated in the scripture above. His encounter with the Lord is one of the greatest documented turning points in the history of humanity. However, this was not a physical vision of God but a revelation of prophetic spiritual understanding of the heart and mind of God concerning the patriarch. There are seven dimensions in this vision which reveal the path to greatness and the manifestation of the glory of God. It is a precursor of the transitory journey of the believer from abasement to eminence. Therefore, this vision is available to every believer, and you must lay hold and appropriate it for your life. This is the vision of God as described to Abram, his future state revealed to him. By this vision, God was preparing the mind of Abram to face the possible challenges that were going to surface in the later chapters of his life. God called Abram and described the seven dimensions of his future state. Abram was to see himself within the context of this vision and it is equally available to you, so you must see yourself through the lens of this vision. Let us review each of these seven dimensions of the vision of greatness given to Abram below.

1. DEPARTURE FROM THE FAMILIAR TERRITORY/ COMFORT ZONE (GET OUT OF YOUR COUNTRY, FROM YOUR FAMILY AND FROM YOUR FATHER'S HOUSE)

In the aforementioned scripture, the first line of God's instruction was for Abram to get out of his country, family, and father's household. The underlying meaning of these three locations is the comfort zone. The comfort zone is defined as "a behavioral state where a person operates in an anxiety-neutral position." (Bardwick, Judith M. 1995) However, another definition from Brené Brown describes it as "Where our uncertainty, scarcity and vulnerability are minimized—where we believe we'll have access to enough love, food, talent, time, admiration. Where we feel we have some control." (Brown, Brene. 2008) The comfort zone is the place where people become comfortable doing what they do and therefore have no desire for change. Those dwelling in their comfort zones find reasons why they cannot or should not change even if the change can be beneficial or positively transformative. The ease of dwelling in a comfort zone is so comforting that most people may not have any impetus for departure. It is said that the comfort zone is so comforting that nothing grows out of there.

> *"The inability to detach oneself from their comfort zone will hinder their ability to achieve the fullness of their potential."*

Naturally, people tend to navigate towards an environment, place, or assignment where they feel safe and comfortable. At the workplaces, people gravitate towards taking assignments they are familiar with or working with colleagues they are comfortable with. Though that is not bad, the inability to detach oneself from their comfort zone will hinder their ability to achieve the fullness of their potential. The first step to the destination of greatness is to gather courage and move from your comfort zone, familiar territory, and area of complacency. These are the three main environments you must commence from to tread on the path to greatness.

Since vision espouses one's future, the first line of transition was for Abram to see himself outside the context of his country, family, and father's household. In other words, Abram needed to see himself outside the comfort zone. God triggered a future state in the mind of Abram where he was dwelling outside this zone - Mesopotamia. God was calling Abram to leave his comfort zone and take up new challenges needed to birth the fullness of his potential.

The first step towards achieving greatness, success, or fulfilling one's vision is to depart from this environment. The study of performance management prescribes the transition from the comfort zone through the fear zone, learning zone, and growth zone before reaching the optimal performance zone. The most challenging of all these zones is the fear zone, which comes right after the comfort zone, making it very difficult or impossible for some people to progress to their vision. Some people have not achieved their vision because they have not been able to dissociate themselves from their comfort zone.

At a point in time, the Israelites had settled in their comfort zone at Mount Sinai and had aborted their desire to inherit the Promised Land. As long as they remained in their comfort zone, the vision of possessing the Promised Land eluded them. God had to call them to break camp and advance (Deuteronomy 1:7 NIV) just as He called Abram to leave his family for a new land.

Secondly, departure from your comfort zone takes you through moments of loneliness. When you understand and decide to pursue your vision, you will have to leave the crowd behind and choose to be lonely to fine-tune the vision. Many people will not believe in your vision and may even part company with you because of their lack of understanding or belief. However, the ability to accept your loneliness is essential to prepare you and helps you to master your vision. You gain more control over your vision during your time alone. It is important that the visionary attains the state of leaving the multitude behind (Mark 4:36 NKJV) to focus on the vision. Remember that once you set yourself to a new destiny, not all friends, loved ones, and family members can undertake that journey with you. Be ready to trade some relationships and friendships for the vision.

Thirdly, departure from the comfort zone may ensure that sources or elements of distraction are blocked from interfering with your vision. Familiar territory or the comfort zone can be a source of distraction as family members and friends may highlight your weaknesses or focus on your inabilities. Out of goodwill and love, families and friends may find ways to "protect" you from "danger." It is against this backdrop that taking a risky path will meet opposition and resistance from loved ones.

Leaving your comfort zone implies leaving sources of distraction behind. In Genesis chapter 22: 6-14 (NKJV), Abraham realized that the vision to sacrifice his beloved son Isaac needed to be executed outside his familiar territory. Can you imagine what would have happened had Abraham attempted to sacrifice Isaac in the presence of loved ones or his family? This is the reason he left everyone behind and journeyed to the place of sacrifice with only Isaac.

The other impediment you abandon by leaving your comfort zone is the possibility of complacency. The manifestation of complacency is so profound in the comfort zone that it is one of the main agents of mediocracy. When people become so familiar with their task, assignment, job, or any endeavor, complacency sets in. Complacency subdues innovation, critical thinking, risk taking, and desire for higher achievement or better experience. The Apostle Paul intentionally did not give room for complacency when he stated in the book of Philippians that "Brethren, I count not myself to have apprehended: but this one thing I do, forgetting those things which are behind, and reaching forth unto those things which are before." Philippians 3:13 (NKJV)

One of the most inspirational and visionary life stories in the twenty-first century is that of Mother Teresa of Calcutta. Her ability to depart from her comfort zone is admirable and may have been one of her secret ingredients of success, which includes winning the Nobel Peace Prize (1979), touching the lives of many, and ultimately, her canonization into sainthood by the Catholic Church. Born **Anjezë Gonxhe Bojaxhiu** , Mother Teresa understood the limitations of dwelling in the comfort zone. At age 18, she felt called by God to leave her native Albania (a departure from the comfort zone) to join the Sisters of Loreto in India, where she served mostly as a teacher for the next twenty years. Having sighted the plight of the poor in the city of Calcutta and through a series of visions, Christ spoke to her about a more personal and direct service towards the suffering poor, and she made the difficult decision of leaving her order (another departure from the comfort zone) to live amongst the needy in the slums of Calcutta. Her departure from her home country of Albania and subsequently from her comfort zone with the Sisters of Loreto to focus on the poorest of the poor is a perfect example of pursuing a vision of greatness by taking the first step of departure from the comfort zone.

Today, God is still calling many to leave their father's household, countries, towns, cities, workplaces, professions, or any other comfort zone to set themselves on the path of greatness..

Personal Testimony

Many years ago, I had a stable and decent career working in the banking sector in the United States of America. My position came with an appreciable level of financial compensation, a clear career path of growth, and a comfortable standard of living. However, my pursuit of rising through the professional ladder was surprisingly correlated with my desire to serve the Lord. I purposely decided to ignore the calling of God, though it had become obvious and the call to avail myself for full-time ministry was intensifying with time. The thought of departing from this respectable position did not make it easy to accept God's calling, and this went on for some years. It took the grace of God, wise counsel from my wife, prayer, and good advice from some leaders before I could finally succumb to the "divine pressure." With the benefit of hindsight, I am eternally grateful that I departed from the comfort zone of corporate America and took the spiritual journey to the unknown land of full-time ministry.

Exhortation

As you continue to read this book, there may be many areas in your life that you feel the inclination of departing from; there are suggestions, personal transitioning advice, and recommendations that may seem uncomfortable to implement. These uncomfortable suggestions are calling you out of your comfort zone to the path of greatness. To the institutional leader, establishing some of these recommendations may expose the inner workings of your organization. This may be extremely uncomfortable but is essential to lifting your organization to the next level of achievement. For example, as a senior minister, delegating authority and sitting under the feet of your spiritual son or daughter can be uncomfortable to many, but may be needed to give you an unfamiliar perspective of ministry. You may have a fervent desire to step out and step up to your vision. I want to challenge you to step out of that comfortable position, job, career, lifestyle, or profession and pursue your vision. Yes, it may be difficult at the beginning, but know that you are cut out for this, and you can make it.

Why Stepping Out?

Stepping out of your comfort zone should not be seen only when momentous events occur. Sometimes this could mean doing trivial things or making small moves. It could mean inviting a co-worker to lunch, initiating a conversation with a stranger, starting a Bible study group with a few neighbors, or inviting a colleague minister to share your pulpit. Every step you take and every uncomfortable move you make is distancing you from familiar territory and setting you apart for greatness. If you are an institutional leader, founder, or administrator, may I encourage you to relinquish some of the roles and responsibilities you find uncomfortable to part with and bring in younger generations for a smooth succession plan.

THE VISION OF GREATNESS (THE ABRAHAMIC VISION)

Like the call of Abram, know that God is calling you to a life of greatness that will ripple through the oceans of generations for a positive impact. Let your vision fuel your desire for new things, get out into the world, start that business, call that friend, start that ministry, write that idea down, move from that town/city/country, and you will be on your way to greatness. You are the Abram of your generation. Hark the voice of vision calling, for your response has an inter-generational impact. Generations are waiting for you, nations are depending on you, families are relying on you, souls are hanging on the pillar of your decision, "for the creation waits in eager expectation for the children of God to be revealed." Romans 8:19 NIV As the deer pants for the water, may your soul long for the realization of that vision.

2. DEPARTURE TO AN UNKNOWN LAND (TO A LAND THAT I WILL SHOW YOU)

The second dimension of the vision to greatness and glory is departure to the unknown land. Fear is the main hallmark of the unknown land. People begin to lose their confidence when they exit their comfort zone, due to the fear of the unknown. The fear of the unknown creates anxiety in the lives of many people with three probable forms of responses: fight (meet the challenge), flight (run away/hide), or freeze (become paralyzed). However, a move to the unknown land is the next line of action after departure from the comfort zone.

"It is certain that every visionary will encounter unknown dimensions and uncharted territories."

Every visionary must accept the fact that you will go through an unknown land and walk through an uncharted territory. Before he could become a great nation with a great name, Abram would have to experience many unknowns. The Christian journey is a walk through and continuous engagement with unknowns. Indeed, the path to your destiny will lead you through unfamiliar or unchartered territories. This means that you should be ready to encounter unfamiliar situations, places, people, and circumstances if you are to achieve your vision. This clarion call to greatness is being echoed in the heart of many leaders, corridors of many organizations, board rooms of many corporations, faculties of many academic institutions, prayer closets of many believers, living rooms of many families, and the pulpit of many churches. To the minister, there are unknown places where souls are eagerly waiting for the manifestation of your ministry (Romans 8:18). No matter how engaging your ministry is with God, there will be some unknowns on the path to your destiny.

What to Observe

Two things to consciously consider on the land of the unknown are:

    a. Do not choose the path of least resistance. (Flight)

    b. Do not quit no matter the magnitude of difficulty. (Freeze)

Be careful that you do not settle on the path of least resistance or take to the flight response. The path of least resistance is choosing the easier way out or running away from the unknown. It is said that hard work never breaks bones; however, it is not uncommon to see many people settling for roles and responsibilities that are easier in their line of action. Determination is a key factor in the achievement of great visions. The lack of determination in any endeavor is a guaranteed recipe for failure. Greatness is not born out of easiness; if it were so, everyone would be great! It is vital to consider all options, including difficult ones; take some calculated risks and sometimes choose the less known option. It is better to employ the factor of determination rather than resting on the shoulders of fear. Remember that there is no easy path to sustainable success.

The other consideration to keep in mind in the land of the unknown is not to quit no matter how challenging the situation may be. Quitting or freezing is the master key to the dwelling place of failure. One of the main challenging issues in the unknown land is uncertainty. The prevalence of uncertainty sometimes makes it exceedingly difficult to go through this stage. The uncertainty in marriage, business, ministry, profession, relocation, traveling, and many more may generate a tornado of stress or anxiety. If not well managed, you may settle on the path of abandonment rather than the pursuit of your vision. Many have admitted defeat and have recoiled to their comfort zone for the burial of their vision due to uncertainty. Doing something is part of the success story, but doing nothing is the first law of failure. If you are walking through your unknown land, still be confident and remember God is with you. For indeed He will never leave you nor forsake you (Isaiah 43:1-4 NKJV).

Purpose of the Unknown

Sometimes, God will intentionally take you through the unknown land for the purpose of achieving the following:

- Dependence on God: One of God's intentions for living in the unknown is to build your full dependency on Him. For the believer, traveling through the unknowns creates a constant state of anticipation and dependency on God.

God called Abram and informed him that he was going to an unknown land. For Abram to successfully dwell in the unknown land, it was particularly important that he fully depend on God's direction, guidance, strategy, and fully rely on Him. This called for an unwavering faith, trust, and confidence in the Lord. God is calling many people to the unknown land. He is calling people to explore a new land in their ministries, marriages, professions, family, and other areas of life. Your dependence on God is your sure way to successfully pass through the unknowns of life.

"The purpose of the unknown is to build our dependency on God, manage expectation and fear."

- Manage Expectation: Sometimes God uses passage through the unknowns to manage expectation. One of the main tasks of a good project manager is the ability to manage both client and project team expectations. It is achieved through setting clear scope, defining tasks, timelines, milestones, identifying potential risks and issues, and communicating progress on a timely basis. The process of going through the unknown is sometimes essential in managing people's expectations. I have mentioned that most spiritual visions are far beyond the imagination of their receiver. Mostly if God should give a full disclosure of visions, many people will not pursue the course. Therefore, God will sometimes stage the release of details at the level and scope you can handle at each point in time.

Kaizen, a Japanese business philosophy, is a term meaning to change for the better or continuous improvement. It focuses on the processes that continuously improve operations, gradually improving productivity, making the working environment more efficient, and promoting all employees' involvement. The area of interest for me here is that, under the Kaizen philosophy, production processes are broken down into multiple tasks ensuring that efficiency is achieved at the task level. Though the goal is to improve upon efficiency in the whole production line, the focus is at the task level. A similar strategy is sometimes seen in the unveiling of visions. To help manage your expectation, God will sometimes reveal only the portion of the vision you can handle. Therefore, it is important you pursue whatever level of detail God has granted to you to help accomplish or realize your full vision.

- Manage Fear: It is said that life begins where fear ends. Fear is one of the greatest weapons that has aborted many visions, turned dreams into nightmares, reduced the great to ordinary, and has taken many unrealized potentials to the grave. God sometimes takes visionaries through the unknowns to manage the potential fear that may arise from apprehending the full scale of the vision. God will sometimes ensure that the full scale of the vision is not laid bare at the onset of conception. The magnitude of some visions is so great, unrealistic, and inconceivable that if God does not stagger its unveiling, the intended recipient may forfeit its pursuit out of fear.

At the onset of 2019, one of my church members called me and requested that I visit him at his office. I obliged and set up a date for the visit. This church member, who had started an investment management firm some years ago, was experiencing challenging situations in the business. Upon my arrival at the business, he recounted the difficulties the business was encountering and his thought of folding up the company for good. With my experience in financial and investment management, I provided some expert advice and prayed with him. During the course of the prayer, the Lord opened my eyes to see a future portfolio value under the management of the company. The amount was so huge, and when I sought permission from the Lord to share the number with him, the Lord declined. The Lord indicated that though that was going to be the value of assets under management in his future portfolio, I should not tell him to avoid the potential of scaring him off. I encouraged and informed him that the Lord had turned the business around so he should maintain his focus and continue to work hard. Every now and then, I will call and share prayers with him and today, he has an incredibly significant asset under management. I still have not disclosed the amount I saw to him, but we continue to pray for its realization. Yes, God did not want to scare him off by revealing the totality of the vision because the gap between the current and future states was so wide that achieving such a vision was almost impossible.

Exhortation

God may be calling you to the land of the unknown. You may have every excuse and tangible reason not to chase that vision, fear may have taken the better part of you, but I am here to inform you that the God of impossibilities is your God. Remember in Ecclesiastes 3:11 NIV, He has made everything beautiful in its time. He has also set eternity in the human heart; yet no one can fathom what God has done from beginning to end. Do not give up, continue to chase after that vision, and one day you will declare, "This is the Lord's doing; it is marvelous in our eyes." Psalm 118:23 NKJV Depend on God, put your trust in Him, maintain your focus on the vision, work with a progressive improvement mindset, and you will get to that destiny.

3. ABRAM (ABRAHAM) THE GREAT NATION (I WILL MAKE YOU A GREAT NATION)

Abraham is considered the father of many nations. Some of these nations include the Israelites, Ishmaelites, Edomites, Amalekites, Kenizzites, Midianites, and the Assyrians. In fact, most of the people in the present-day Middle East and all Jews globally identify Abraham as their ancestor. That magnitude of affiliation is a dimension of greatness implied in God's covenant. The significance of God's promise is better appreciated when we consider the timing of the vision. At the time God gave him the vision of greatness, Abraham was living with a barren woman. However, God was transitioning Abraham's vision from focusing on the barrenness to seeing himself as the father of many nations. It is like logging into an overdrawn bank account only to be told that you will be a millionaire. It was inconceivable, but Abraham still believed that with God all things were possible. Later, in Genesis 13:14–18 NKJV, God's progressive revelation came to bear when He showed Abraham a more detailed version of his greatness. Here, God asked Abraham to lift his eyes and see to the north, south, east and west. The extent he could see would provide the spectrum of his greatness. In other words, the scope of Abraham's vision will determine the dimension of his greatness. Further unveiling of Abraham's vision was that his descendants will be as numerous as the dust of the earth. The childless old man living with a barren menopausal wife was going to have innumerable descendants? The audacity of faith, indeed!

Expansion of the Covenant

God continued to broaden the scope of Abraham's vision as follows: In Genesis 13 and 15, God told him that his descendants would be like the innumerable dust of the earth and the stars in the sky. A combination of the two visions indicates that God gave Abraham visual aids to help him see the vision round the clock; the sand at the seashore was visible during the day, and the stars in the heavens were visible at night. God had set before Abraham an undeniable vision in a form of visual aid to propel and sustain his faith during the day and at night.

Little Beginning, Great Ending

In Genesis 13:17, God instructed Abraham to arise and walk. The beginning of every greatness is small, so the Bible admonishes that "For who has despised the day of small things? For these seven rejoice to see, The plumb line in the hand of Zerubbabel. They are the eyes of the Lord, Which scan to and fro throughout the whole earth." Zachariah 4:10 NKJV No level of greatness has been achieved overnight. Every great person, company, church, institution, nation, marriage, and endeavor started small. God is interested in seeing you start the business, launching the vision, enrolling in that school, registering that business, investing with that one dollar, and just starting. Take consistently small steps towards the vision and it is only a matter of time before you arrive at your destination. The greatest novel started with one word, the greatest church started with one soul, the mightiest company stated with one product, the best chef started with one meal, the longest journey started with one step, the biggest ocean started with one drop of water, the greatest surgeon started with one incision, the most successful marketer started with one sale, and the most powerful prayer warrior started with one prayer. All you need to achieve greatness is to consistently make one move at a time towards the vision. Indeed, it takes just a step to head towards greatness. Sometimes we observe greatness from the lens of completeness, but that is not what God is interested in. Abraham's achievement of greatness was solidified when he took the first step out of his country, people, and father's household. This first step is usually the most difficult and requires deep faith (Luke 17:6 NIV).

The greatness of Abraham was not going to occur in a big leap. It is said that Rome was not built in a day. Every remarkable success is an accumulation of little efforts that may not even be seen or appreciated, but over a period, they accumulate to enormous success. This is called the law of incremental success or the law of accumulation. These tiny little efforts start to accumulate like a snowball and build up over time and over the years. This is the dimension in which Abrahamic greatness was going to unfold.

Exhortation

Today, God is calling someone to the destiny of greatness and all that you need to do is to take that first step, then the second, the third, and very soon, you will be at the pedestal of prominence. Yes indeed, you may not have that level of education, network, experience, money, background, expertise, or influence, but God is still saying it is possible. God is looking for partners like Abraham to make them great for the glorification of His name. This promise is for you and your descendants. No matter how insignificant you may perceive your step, still come on board, and let us fly to the altitude of global visibility.

4. ABRAM (ABRAHAM) THE BLESSED ONE
(I WILL BLESS YOU)

The fourth dimension of Abraham's vision was that he needed to see himself swimming in and drinking from the streams of God's blessings. Abraham was going to be blessed by God. The fundamental meaning of blessing is being able to have an intimate relationship with and access to God. This level of access may sometimes manifest in the provision of material possession. The blessings of God can be categorized as spiritual and physical blessings; however, in most cases, the spiritual blessings inform the manifestation of the physical blessings. God is the provider of every good thing; the Bible says "Every good and perfect gift is from above, coming down from the Father of the heavenly lights, who does not change like shifting shadows." James 1:17 NIV To have an intimate relationship with God is to be granted access to the very secret place of the Almighty. The blessings of Abraham are detailed in Genesis 17:2-8 and Deuteronomy 28:1-13. These material manifestations are because of spiritual access granted to Abraham through his faithfulness to God. The focus is not the material manifestation but the spiritual position, which eventually grants us access to all realms including the material or physical. The Lord promised to bless Abraham and make him the father of many nations, make him exceedingly fruitful, to keep His intergenerational covenant, and to give his descendants the land He showed him for an everlasting possession (Genesis 17:4-8 NIV). In Genesis 22:17 AMP, the Lord told Abraham that, "In blessing I will bless you and in multiplying I will multiply your descendants like the stars of the heavens and like the sand on the seashore. And your Seed (Heir) will possess the gate of His enemies."

Blessing through Jesus Christ

Jesus Christ is a descendant of Abraham and is now the pathway to spiritual access for the believer (John 14:6 NIV). Therefore, the call to seek first the kingdom of God and His righteousness is the key to greatness. This is because when we become members of the Kingdom we have access to the goodness in the Kingdom, which sometimes may manifest in material provision through divine providence (Matthew 6:33 NIV). The material blessings can be assessed by the believer who lives in obedience to the statues, precepts, and laws of the Lord.

Many people equate blessings to material possessions. It is not uncommon to see people flaunting their wealth as a sign of their blessings. Though material possessions could be a manifestation of God's blessings, true blessings are not so much of what you have but the source or provider of what you have. The understanding of God's blessings is that your gains are a result of your intimate relationship with Him. No matter your level of attainment in life, you must always acknowledge the source of this enablement. It is humbling to admit your inability to attain those statuses by your own strength but only through your access to our Lord and Savior Jesus Christ. Divine providence is only one aspect of God's manifested blessings.

5. ABRAM (ABRAHAM) THE GREAT NAME (AND MAKE YOUR NAME GREAT)

Your name is a representation of you. Inherent in everyone's name is the totality of that person's character, authority, and personality. Your name is an expression of your identity and creates an image or perception of you in the minds of people. The mention of the name Mr. Bean (a popular British comedian) brings laughter to the faces of many. Nelson Mandela denotes selfless political leadership. Dr. Kwame Nkrumah represents a champion of anti-colonialism while Lionel Messi takes people's minds straight to the football/soccer field. From Genesis chapter 12 through 16, the original name Abram was used. No matter the level of engagement between God and Abram, the promised blessings of God were not materialized until his name was eventually changed in Chapter 17. "Neither shall thy name any more be called Abram, but thy name shall be Abraham; for a father of many nations have I made thee."

Genesis 17:5 (KJV) The change of his name to Abraham had now positioned him to receive the blessing of becoming the father of many nations.

> *"Inherent in everyone's name is the totality of that person's character, authority and personality."*

Jacob's Name Change

In Genesis 32:22-32 NKJV, the Bible gives an account of how Jacob wrestled with the angel all night before his name was changed to Israel. The angel gave Jacob the new name Israel to mark a turning point in his life. Jacob had been in training up to that point, but now he had to get down to the business of being a patriarch. The name Israel "One who prevails with God" or "Let God prevail" came out of a struggle, commitment, and unrelenting effort to receive the blessings of God. Jacob's act of exchanging soup for the birthright of Esau, tricking his father for the blessings, and outwitting his uncle Laban for his property did not yield the desired results. However, his all-night wrestling with the angel and subsequent name change positioned him to become one of the patriarchs of Israel. His name change from Jacob to Israel was essential for the manifestation and fulfillment of the covenant of God.

Authority in the Name Jesus Christ

In Philippians 2:9-11 NKJV, the name Jesus Christ is revealed to be above all other names; therefore, at the mention of the name Jesus, its inherent authority compels every name to submit. The name Jesus Christ is a great name and embodies spiritual authority, power, and victory. Indeed, powers of darkness, sicknesses, diseases, spiritual authority, and everything that has a name must submit to the authority in the name Jesus Christ. Every name is called to obedience at the mention of the name Jesus Christ. That is the level of authority available to Christians whose acts and deeds are truly in line with the word of God and whose character truly represents that of Christ.

Divine name change does not occur unexpectedly; it is always preceded and triggered by an event. Abraham's name change emerged out of his obedience to the Lord, Jacob's name change occurred out of his commitment and struggle for the blessings, and the authority in the name Jesus Christ was born out of humility. Those who desire to have meaningful, impactful, blessed names must adhere to a course worthy of emulation.

I was informed that my name "Amuzu" literally means "the lagoon has prevailed over the sea." Thus, the name is an embodiment of resilience, strength, and inherent power for victory over any kind and type of opposition (irrespective of its magnitude). Many times, when I am faced with a strong opposition or major obstacle in life, I recall not only my position as a Christian but also the meaning of my name. This has inspired me on many occasions to face and prevail over life's oppositions and challenges. The meaning of names is incredibly significant and mostly has direct bearing on certain character exhibition of the bearer.

Many are seeking great names but may not be ready for the level of commitment and sacrifice that comes with it. Per the law of exchange, nothing good comes on a silver platter. You must give something to receive something. Many young people idolize some celebrities due to their accomplishments and hail the names of great men and women in their field of aspiration. There is nothing wrong with that, but what they may not be privileged to know is that these great names may have been born out of many years of sacrifice, commitment, obedience, self-discipline, self-development, and investment. So, whether you aspire for a personal or organizational great name, you must remember that it comes at a cost. The secret is to consistently embark on developmental or value-added activities for yourself or your organization. Value-added activities could mean investing your time to acquire the knowledge and skills relevant in your field of aspiration. The bottom line is that great names do not just happen; they are worked for! If your vision is a great name, be ready to sacrifice and work for it.

6. ABRAM (ABRAHAM) THE CHANNEL OF BLESSING (AND YOU SHALL BE A BLESSING. I WILL BLESS THOSE WHO BLESS YOU, AND IN YOU ALL THE FAMILIES OF THE EARTH SHALL BE BLESSED)

The sixth dimension of Abrahamic vision is that he needed to see himself as a conduit of God's blessings unto humanity. The blessings of Abraham were not just for him and his descendants but for people who will network with him, bless him, or invariably wish him well, and through him every family on earth was to receive their blessing. Abraham was mandated to become a channel of blessing to humanity. The manifestation of Abraham's blessing is not only about material possessions but also includes access to God, good health, peace of mind, riches in material and non-material terms. However, this does not mean that believers in Christ cannot be rich and materially wealthy. But it doesn't happen simply because you believe in Jesus Christ. You will have to work your way to the increase (Ephesians 4:28 NIV; 1 Thessalonians 4:11-12 NIV; 2 Thessalonians 3:10-13 NIV). The three composi-

THE VISION OF GREATNESS (THE ABRAHAMIC VISION)

tions of the sixth dimension of Abrahamic blessings are as follows:

a. And you shall be a blessing: According to this declaration, Abraham was going to be a source of blessing to other people. He was going to be blessed to the extent that this blessing could impact the lives of those whom he may decide. This is a dependency blessing, where the lives of others are impacted positively due to the decision of people they may depend on. A typical case is that of children and parents. Some children are blessed through the blessed position of their parents.

b. I will bless those who bless you: Those who network with him or decide to associate with him could also receive the blessings from the Lord. This is called blessing by association. This started with the manifestation of Lot's blessings. As long as Lot was associated with Abraham, he was blessed with livestock, servants, and slaves. His dissociation meant a termination from his source of blessing.

c. And in you all the families of the earth shall be blessed: Finally, those who accept the God of Abraham could receive the blessings of Abraham. The blessing of Abraham is extended to all humanity through the work of our Lord Jesus Christ. Accepting Jesus Christ as your Lord and personal Savior positions you in the paradigm of Abrahamic blessings. This is because Jesus Christ is the seed (Genesis 22:18 NKJV) of Abraham, the source and conduit of the new covenant blessings. By this promise, gentiles have now become equal partakers of the blessings of the Lord. Just as Abraham was called from his family by the Lord and offered an opportunity through a covenant, gentiles have also been called out of their families and offered the opportunity of blessings through the death and resurrection of our Lord Jesus Christ, which is the new and everlasting covenant. Let me emphasize that just as Abrahamic (and other Old Testament) covenants served as the basis for the blessings of the Jews, the new and everlasting covenant now serves as the basis for the blessings of gentiles. "Be mindful of His covenant forever, the promise which He commanded and established to a thousand generations, The covenant which He made with Abraham, and His sworn promise to Isaac. He confirmed it as a statute to Jacob, and to Israel for an everlasting covenant." (1 Chronicles 16:15-17 AMP) Therefore, through the seed of Abraham, i.e., Jesus Christ, all the families of the earth can now access the blessings that were hitherto reserved of the Jews (Galatians 3:14 NIV). The basis for the inheritance of these promises is our acceptance of Jesus Christ as our Lord and Savior and our faith in the Word of the Lord. Deuteronomy 28:1- 13 NKJV enumerates the blessings of obedience which invariably are the blessings we receive for being obedient to the word of God.

7. ABRAM (ABRAHAM) THE SOURCE OF CURSE: (AND I WILL CURSE HIM WHO CURSES YOU)

This scripture is one of the most dangerous proclamations of the Lord concerning his servant Abraham and by extension Christians. It is an indication of the level of protection the Lord was willing to offer Abraham and his descendants. So what is a curse? It is an invocation of a supernatural power to traverse a negative impact on a person or to harm somebody. Since the Lord is and has the ultimate power, this scripture implies that He would invoke His own power to negatively impact or harm anyone who desires or intends to harm Abraham. This invocation of power to harm people will be the default position of those who seek to harm Abraham and therefore his descendants.

We see a glimpse of this position when Pharaoh tried to take Sarah as his wife. The Lord came to Abraham's defense by bringing unusual sickness to Pharaoh and his household. The curses of disobedience are listed in Deuteronomy 28:15-68 for our review and reflection.

THE VISION OF GREATNESS (THE ABRAHAMIC VISION)

Chapter Summary

- The Vision of Greatness: Many people and organizations harbor and nurture the desire for greatness. Unfortunately, such desires do not materialize due to various reasons. Below are seven dimensions to greatness as enshrined in scripture using Abrahamic vision as a model.

    - Departure from the Familiar Territory/Comfort Zone: The first step toward the destination of greatness is departure from the comfort zone. The comfort zone is the place or state of life where people are so content with what they are doing that they have no desire for change. Departure from your comfort zone implies departure from familiarity, and complacency. After the comfort zone comes the fear zone, learning zone, growth zone, and optimal performance zone.

    - Departure to Unknown Land: The unknown land is a place of uncertainty and no familiarity. Fear of the unknown is the main hallmark of this land and calls for dependency on the Lord. Expectations are managed on the land of the unknown.

    - Abram (Abraham) the Great Nation: Every believer has been called to a life of greatness; however, the beginning of every greatness is small. No level of greatness is achieved overnight or presented on a silver platter. The path to greatness is consistent small steps towards a vision that results in an accumulated significant difference over time.

    - Abram (Abraham) the Blessed One: Believers are the blessed ones. The fundamental meaning of blessings is the ability to have direct access and intimate relationship with God. Attainment of this position opens the door for God's goodness, which may manifest in material possessions, good health, long life, etc.

- Abram (Abraham) the Great Name: Inherent in a name is the totality of a person's character, authority, and personality. A name is an expression of an identity. Great names do not come without effort, but are attained through triggers like sacrifice, prudence, hard work, commitment, and diligence.

- Abram (Abraham) the Channel of Blessing: Though Abraham was called to be a channel of blessings to humanity, that calling is not only reserved for Abraham. All Christians are called to become channels of God's blessings onto humanity.

- Abram (Abraham) the Source of Curse: A curse is an invocation of supernatural power to traverse a negative impact on a person or to harm someone. Abraham's attainment of greatness was accompanied by an invocation of great spiritual opposition against his enemies. This was a form of protection the Lord accorded His servant for his obedience.

CHAPTER THIRTEEN

THE VISION OF SUCCESS (NEHEMIAH'S VISION)

"(THE FIRST STEP OF EVERY SUCCESSFUL JOURNEY OCCURS IN THE MIND."- Godfred Dodzie Amuzu)

> *"One night the Lord spoke to Paul in a vision: 'Do not be afraid; keep on speaking, do not be silent. For I am with you, and no one is going to attack and harm you, because I have many people in this city.'"*
> **Acts 18:9-10 NIV**

VISION STORY- KOFI ANNAN

Regarded as the finest international diplomat to ever grace the face of the earth, co-recipient of 2001 Nobel Peace Prize, an internationally acclaimed transformative leader, recipient of countless honorary degrees and awards, Kofi Annan was the seventh secretary general of the United Nations from 1997 to 2006 and the first secretary general to emerge from the ranks of United Nations staff. Kofi Annan was born in Kumasi, Ghana, on 8 April 1938, and was fluent in English, French, and several African languages. His rise to the apex of global leadership was fueled by his vision to promote and establish global peace, human rights, the rule of law, and ending deadly diseases such as AIDS, tuberculosis, and malaria.

He executed this vision through the revitalization of the United Nations, including strengthening the organization's management, coherence and accountability, and massive investments in training and technology. He also pursued the introduction of a new whistleblower policy and financial disclosure requirements, increased the number of personnel and operations, and implemented steps aimed at improving coordination at the country level, thereby making the international system more effective. Kofi Annan's unrivaled achievement and remarkable international successes is a great legacy fueled by an inspiring vision.

INTRODUCTION

"Success is predictable based on certain indicators, rules of engagement and lifestyle."

Many people aspire to be successful in life or in their areas of endeavor; however, some of these aspirations do not materialize simply because sometimes, the fundamental elements of success are not known or understood. Success is a cumulative measure of achievements and engagements over a period of time. Unfortunately, many people meet the criteria of engagements without the outcome of achievements. All too often, we meet and know people who are seriously engaged in pursuing their vision or goal but have little or nothing to show as achievement. The path of success is well defined, so that those who have the right knowledge and understanding can easily envision the outcome of their endeavors right from the start. In fact, success is very predictable based on certain indicators, rules of engagement, and lifestyles. Most people who have passed through the path of success can predict ability to succeed based on the rules I'm going to treat below.

I will be using the story in the book of Nehemiah to elaborate on the pathway of success, which is equally applicable to almost every area and dimensions of life. I have intentionally chosen the book of Nehemiah because inherently, this story represents one of the most profoundly successful stories in the history of humanity (Nehemiah Chapters 1-13). The dimensions, magnitude, speed (timeline), quality, impact, and sustenance of the vision from conception through implementation present an ideal case for our studies and opportunity for emulation. There are many success-bound rules and guidelines inherent in this story, which resulted in a radical change in the lives of the people. Applying these rules in politics, ministry, academia, entertainment, business, charity, and any area of life will produce a guaranteed successful outcome. Anyone with a vision for success must understand and apprehend the meaning of these rules or guidelines, which I have categorized as the orbit of success. I can guarantee you success if you diligently and faithfully follow and implement these guidelines below.

1. PROBLEM- (NEHEMIAH 1:2-3 NIV, 1 SAMUEL 17 NKJV)

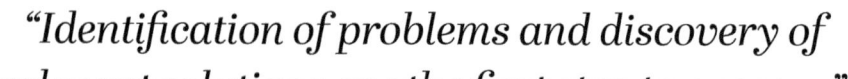

"Identification of problems and discovery of relevant solutions are the first step to success."

The first orbit of success is the identification of problems. Everyone who desires to succeed in life must first seek to identify problem(s) in society, workplace, or area of jurisdiction. Problems breed pain in people's lives, therefore, identifying the problem means discovering the source of pain. Once you discover people's

THE VISION OF SUCCESS (NEHEMIAH'S VISION)

source of pain, commit to finding a way to soothe, alleviate or minimize the magnitude of the pain through the provision of a solution. The solution must be the answer to the problem, and this can be packaged as a product or service to the market or to the people affected by the problem.

Using the story in the book of Nehemiah, we realize that Nehemiah identified a major problem when he received this news: "They said to me, 'Those who survived the exile and are back in the province are in great trouble and disgrace. The wall of Jerusalem is broken down, and its gates have been burned with fire.'" Nehemiah 1:3 NIV. By this information, Nehemiah realized that the safety and security of the people living in Jerusalem had been compromised, exposing them to potential violence and possibly fatal engagement with their enemies. The problem of compromised safety and security had become an uncomfortable source of pain to the people (thus great affliction and reproach) and needed an urgent solution. Through the news, Nehemiah identified the problem, discovered the source of pain, and sought to present a solution in the form of services by motivating the people to rebuild the walls of Jerusalem and restore the burnt gates.

Those who seek to be successful in every endeavor must develop the affinity and build the courage of seeking solutions to encountered problems. Problems are potential seeds of success; unfortunately, many people would rather abandon any path with problems than master the courage to face them. Understanding the problem is the key to providing a solution.

Successful people are able to identify problems and provide solutions. Whatever area of life you are engaged in, your key to success starts with identifying the problem in that area, understanding the problem, and devising a solution to counter the effect of those problems. This is a fundamental rule of success in every area of life; therefore, if you are in an institution or organization and identify a problem, do not be burdened by the effect of such problems, but rather, seek for understanding and come up with a solution. Once you have the solution, people will gravitate towards you for the solution and may potentially be ready and willing to pay for the solution. I want you to take a few minutes and reflect on your community, church, nation, organization, or institution. Have you identified a problem? If yes, write it down and pursue a path of solution to those problems. Eventually if you discover any solution, package it as either a product or service back to those who are impacted by the problem. Those who can do this have already set themselves on the path of success. See the problems that come your way as opportunities for success rather than a recipe for failure.

Whereas many people will naturally run away from problems, Nehemiah was courageous enough to run towards the problem. Whether you are a student, entrepreneur, parent, civil servant, professor, minister, or volunteer, your ability to *solve* problems will determine and define your level of success. This is why a proper system of education seeks to produce problem solvers. Such people are agents of change who contribute positively towards growth and development in their areas of endeavor. To be positioned for success, the acquisition of knowledge must equally translate towards the development of skills for problems identification and provision of solution.

Vision Diagram

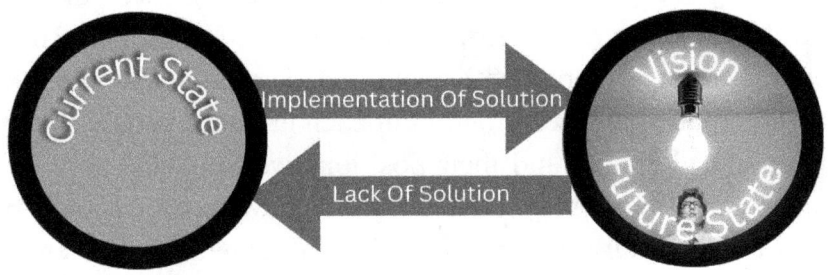

2. PRAYER: (NEHEMIAH 1:4-11 NIV)

The second orbit of success is prayer. Subsequent to the identification of the problem, Nehemiah consulted God and sought divine direction for potential solutions and the way forward. He fasted and prayed earnestly to God, confessing his sins, those of his brethren, and those of his ancestors. He prayed to God for forgiveness. Certain problems may be so overwhelming that only divine intervention can bring a solution. For some problems, the solution is just proper application of knowledge. Therefore, some solutions are prayed to be while others are worked to be. To be successful, one must always recognize and acknowledge the power of divine help without discounting the proper application of knowledge. By consulting God, Nehemiah recognized his inability to pursue a solution by himself, his dependence on God, and submission to the authority of God.

3. PEOPLE

The third orbit of success is to recognize, identify, and appreciate the roles of the PEOPLE. There is no success story devoid of people. In other words, people form the centerpiece and the

THE VALOR OF VISION

foundation of every success story. The presence of people may affect your vision either positively or negatively. Therefore, not recognizing the people appropriately and placing them in their rightful position may be detrimental to the success of the vision. Every vision may interact with about five (5) categories of people. The role, impact, and contribution of each group of people should be properly identified and their positions well noted. These five categories of people have their unique roles, and thus should be treated appropriately in order to derive full benefit from them or avert any potential negative impact. The five categories of people are as follows: the visionary, those in authority, the vision partners, vision beneficiaries, and people in opposition. Let us analyze the potential impact of these groups in detail and determine how to rightfully treat each group to guarantee your success.

- **3.1 THE VISIONARY: Nehemiah 1:4 NIV.** The first person to interact with any vision is the receiver or conceiver of the vision, otherwise known as the visionary. The visionary becomes the main brain, owner, inspiration, and driver of the vision. As the first entity of conviction, he/she holds the key to the successful implementation but may also be the channel for the manifestation of failure. He must be the anchor throughout all the phases and the implementation process. Removal, eliminating, or sidelining the visionary during the execution of any vision exponentially increases the probability of its failure.

  On August 2, 2018, Apple (AAPL) attained a remarkable feat and made history by becoming the world's first publicly traded company to achieve a market capitalization of $1 trillion. It was founded on April 1, 1976, by Steve Jobs (the blazing visionary), Steve Wozniak, and Ronald Wayne (the shy genius executing his vision). Job's 42 year-journey to becoming the lone member of the trillion-dollar club did not occur on a straight path. Four years after being founded, in 1980, Apple's profitability was enviable and was listed as a publicly traded company. In 1983, John Scully was added to Apple as an executive. In 1985, Jobs' fiery, blazing, combative visionary style did not sit well with the board of directors, and he was ousted in favor of Scully. As it turned out, ousting the visionary set the company on a downward spiral. When Jobs returned in 1996, the company had been run down and was not in good shape. However, the return of the visionary revamped the elements and soul of the vision, turning the fortunes of Apple from the brink of bankruptcy to a trillion-dollar company in twenty-two years. I shared the story of Apple to emphasize the importance of the visionary in the execution of any vision.

In reference to the vision of success, Nehemiah the visionary was fully involved throughout the phases of the project, ensuring that the vision was executed successfully. Anytime he departed, he returned to discover that leaders had deviated from the core values and principles he sought to instill and enforce. The role of the visionary in unveiling and bringing clarity to the vision, being the inspiration, force, and brain behind its progress, and providing direction and leadership towards the successful implementation cannot be overemphasized. This role is absolutely essential in the realization of any vision and must be recognized as such.

- **3.2 PEOPLE IN AUTHORITY: Nehemiah 2:2-9 NKJV.** The second category of people to recognize in order to succeed in every venture are those in authority or those who have authority over the visionary. Building and maintaining a sound relationship with people in authority is vital for every success story, though there are some few exceptions to this rule. Nehemiah 2:2-9 NIV recounts the conversation between Nehemiah and the king. He respected the authority of the king and the queen and was submissively honest with them. He sought their permission to leave his post, their backing to travel through the Trans-Euphrates, their authority for security and provisions, and their blessings for a successful mission. Establishing and maintaining a good working relationship with those in authority is extremely vital for the realization of one's vision and achievement of success.

Submission, respect, obedience, and honoring those in authority is a prescription from the scriptures that can easily be applied even in the secular world (Romans 13:1-7 NKJV; 1 Peter 5:5 NIV; Ephesians 6:1-3 NIV). Making your respectful submission towards authority will set the tone for receiving favor and permission. Sometimes, people pride themselves against those in authority based on their level of formal education, experience, background, network, supposed power, or other elements of achievement. There are countless occasions where "spiritual sons and daughters" have rebelled against their mothers and fathers in their quest to establish independent ministries or tread on a new path of spiritual growth. It is important for young prospective ministers of the gospel, who may be more gifted in certain areas of ministry than their mentors, to consciously create a welcoming and spiritually enriching environment for proper dialogue and engagement with their superiors. It is through such an environment that spiritual nuggets are transferred and the lessons of experience unveiled. There is no benefit in any act of rebellion, whether in the Christian or secular world. To the young aspiring ministers of gospel, make it a point to receive the blessings and honorable discharge from your spiritual parents before you depart to pursue your own path of ministry. The value of honorable discharge cannot be quantified and mostly is needful to ensure long term ministerial success. It is advisable not to burn bridges, since you never know which one will be needed to cross over to the land of success. Therefore, no matter your area of business, organization, position, or undertaking, always recognize and appreciate the value of authority, for you have not learned how to work with authority until you learn how to work under authority. The nuggets and wisdom of every profession or business are easily transmitted through the communication line of respect and honor. Creating an environment of respect and honor towards your superior will elicit favor, trust, and repose of confidence.

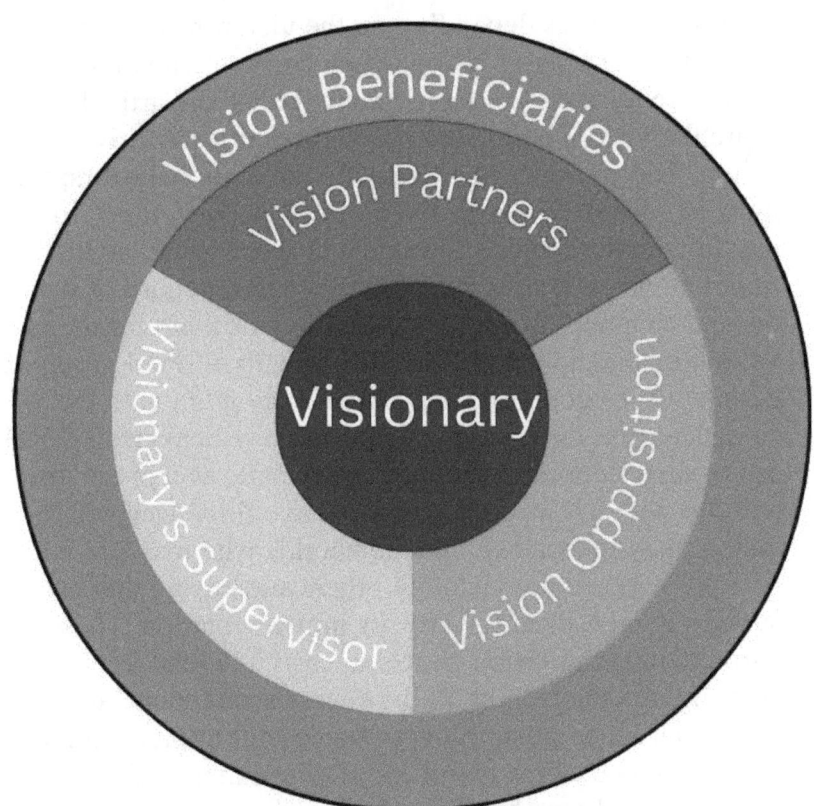

Vision Human Interactions

3.3 THE VISION PARTNERS (Nehemiah 2:12 NKJV)
The third category of people to be mindful of are the VISION PARTNERS. Vision partners are those who help and facilitate the achievement of a vision. They are usually the early believers who may buy into a vision in its infancy, provide support or guidance to the visionary, and play an advisory role. Upon his return to Jerusalem, Nehemiah

identified the vision partners, which he termed as "a few others." (Nehemiah 2:12 NIV). The role of vision partners is indispensable in the implementation of the corporate type of vision; however, for individual vision their level of importance varies depending on the vision-bearer, environment, and the type of vision. Most corporate/institutional visions require the bearer to create the vision, articulate and share the vision, build support, and relentlessly drive the vision. The vision partners may be the early believers; they must be identified and be the focus of the visionary. To successfully drive a vision through a corporation or an institution, the vision-bearer must identify this category of workers and channel his initial energy towards them for their validation and approval. They are usually a small group of people whose goals and aspirations may align with the vision. They are the heralds of the vision (Habakkuk 2:2 NIV) or the early adopters who may appreciate, accept the vision, and run with it. Once the partners have fully accepted the vision, they in turn become the heralds who may run with it. They will sell the vision to others and ensure that enough support is mobilized towards its implementation. These partners help the vision-bearer to carry the load of the vision, lighten the weight on the bearer's shoulders, and provide other kinds of support for successful implementation. The partners become members of your inner circle who may guide you and may be counted on during challenging times.

The level of importance of vision partners varies in an individual-type of vision and may depend on the environment and the vision-bearer. However, identifying and accepting the support of vision partners can be very beneficial to the implementation of one's vision. They may be your support in times of difficulty, or could be the source of encouragement and funding toward successful implementation. Identify such people in your life—some may be your mentors, family members, friends, or even colleagues. They genuinely support the vision, and their contribution can be invaluable. Every visionary must be intentional in identifying these partners, accept their involvement and learn to take their offer to enhance your success.

- **3.4 VISION BENEFICIARIES:** The fourth category of people to consider for successful implementation of every vision is the vision beneficiaries, or what is termed "customers" in the business world. They are those who will derive direct benefit from the implementation and the execution of the vision. The implementation of every vision must benefit someone or some people. These are the people whose "pains" are alleviated or minimized through the utilization of the solution. Understanding this category of people is essential to knowing and constructing the right solution. They may be individuals or organizations who may use the product or services provided through the vision implementation.

  Businesses commit remarkable amounts of resources researching to understand and determine the behavioral pattern of the vision beneficiaries. Whatever your vision is, one paramount factor of success is to know and understand the vision beneficiaries. If your vision is in providing spiritual solutions, try to understand those who will benefit from such solutions. This is equally applicable if you are seeking social, political, business, academic success, or any field of life.

  Implementation of Nehemiah's vision benefited the inhabitants of Jerusalem at the time, as their safety and security were restored through the rebuilding of the walls and repairs of the gates. Getting the beneficiaries to be involved either directly or indirectly is a vital strategy for success. Thus, to be successful in business, devise ways to involve your customers in the design, development, and improvement of the product or services. Consideration and integration of customers' or beneficiaries' feedback is necessary to improve upon the product or services in any field of business.

Successful visionaries understand the importance of continuous engagement with beneficiaries of their vision. Successful presidents must understand the needs and plight of their citizens. In the same way, to be a successful businessperson, you must understand and know the needs of your customers. A successful man or woman of God must comprehend both the spiritual and physical needs of their followers. It is incumbent on successful academic institutions to know the needs of the society they serve. You cannot just ignore the vision beneficiaries or customers and expect to succeed. The vision beneficiaries must be the foundation, focus, and the cylinder around which the door of solution revolves. Their acceptance and utilization of the solution evolving out of the vision is a determination of the success of the vision.

"Every vision has opposition irrespective of how helpful or transformative the vision is."

- **3.5 VISION OPPOSITION:** The fifth category of people to consider on your path to success are those in opposition. Every vision has its opposition. No matter how helpful and transformative the vision is, there will always be opposition. That is human nature—no journey of success has been achieved without opposition. Successful marriages, businesses, leaders, churches, charitable organizations, sporting clubs, nations, and individuals have had their fair share of opposition. In fact, some levels of success are determined based on one's ability to subdue opposition. For example, success in sports hinges on a team's ability to face and overcome opposing teams. To be successful in a democratic election, a political party must be able to face and overcome an opposing party

THE VISION OF SUCCESS (NEHEMIAH'S VISION)

through civil engagements and balloting. Overcoming an opposition as a measure of success transcends multiple dimensions of human life; therefore, anyone who aspires for success in any field must be cognizant of this group of people.

Triggers of opposition could be from lack of understanding, vision, jealousy, miscommunication, or a strategic plan of distraction. Some people just cannot support anything good or may even lack vision for achievement. Some opposition may arise out of evil intention towards either the vision-bearer or the vision beneficiaries.
When the news about the vision of Nehemiah got to Jerusalem and its surroundings, it attracted the interest of Sanballat, the governor of Samaria, and Tobiah, an Ammonite official (Nehemiah 2:10 NIV). The news that someone had come to seek the welfare of the children of Israel grieved Sanballat and Tobiah exceedingly. They took an opposing position and started mobilizing people against the vision and work of Nehemiah. They brought Geshem the Arabian to their camp and strategically tried to discourage the people by laughing and despising the very work meant to restore their safety and security (Nehemiah 2:19 NIV). Subsequently, the news spread through the province that the work of rebuilding the walls of Jerusalem was progressing steadily and this ignited the anger of Sanballat, which caused him to engage the army of Samaria. Tobiah then adopted an insult, speaking negativity, lies, and other strategies to discourage and intimidate the workers (Nehemiah 4:1-3 NIV).

The progression of opposition kept on increasing in correlation to the progress of the work. When it became apparent that the rebuilding of the walls had gone ahead and that the gaps were being closed, the anger of the opposition magnified and the mobilization effort against the work intensified. Now the opposition team had grown to include Sanballat, Tobiah, the Arabs, the Ammonites, and the people of Ashdod (Nehemiah 4:7 NIV).

After the walls were rebuilt and the gaps closed, the enemies resorted to direct confrontational strategy in an attempt to intimidate and stall the progress. They deployed the weapon of lies against the leaders and continued to mobilize more people against the realization of the vision (Nehemiah 6:1-8 NKJV). When Nehemiah and his team prevailed against this strategy, the intensity of opposition was escalated to utilize spiritual tactics. The enemies hired seemingly spiritual people to present a false spiritual solution that they hoped would lead to Nehemiah abandoning the vision, his name being discredited, and the safety and security of the people being compromised again. Eventually they employed the services of a false prophet as the opposition transitioned from physical to the spiritual realm. (Nehemiah 6:10-14 NKJV).

When the enemy had deployed all forms of strategies but none prevailed, the moment of victory materializes. At this stage the fear that they intended to unleash against the vision comes back to them and they begin to lose their self-confidence (Nehemiah 6:16 NIV). This progression of opposition applies to many areas of life.

I have analyzed the progress of vision and the possible corresponding opposition for better understanding in the table below. For the purpose of identification, the opposition moved from external sources, through internal entities, and eventually settled on spirituality. Therefore, possible types of opposition are internal and external; however, for spiritual organizations such as churches, nations, and institutions, the presence of spiritual opposition cannot be underestimated or ignored. Any visionary leader seeking for success must be fully aware of these types of opposition and learn how to deal with them. Understanding and knowing their possible impact and the right strategy to deal with them is a vital component for any success story. I will treat these types of opposition below.

	PROGRESS OF VISION OPPOSITION			
NO	VISION PROGRESS	OPPOSITION REACTION	ADVERSARIES	SCRIPTURE
1	Nehemiah seeks the welfare of Israel	• Adversaries are grieved/ deeply disturbed by the move to seek the welfare of Israel	Sanballat (Horonite) and (Tobiah) Ammonite	Nehemiah 2:10
2	A consensus is reached among the people and a decision to pursue the vision is made; preparation is embarked on.	• Adversaries laugh at and despise the people. • Adversaries question the intention of the people • Adversaries misinterpret the good intention	Sanballat (Horonite), (Tobiah) Ammonite and Geshem (Arabian)	Nehemiah 2:18-19

3	Rebuilding of the wall starts. The initiation of the vision.	• Adversaries are furious, indignant, and mock the people • Adversaries begin to mobilize full support against the vision and seek the service of fighters • Adversaries express concern over the implementation of the vision • Begin to question the ability of the people to complete the work and timeline for completion	Sanballat (Horonite), (Tobiah) Ammonite, Geshem (Arabian), Army of Samaria	Nehemiah 4:1-3
4	The wall is built halfway and joined together. The vision is implemented halfway.	• Adversaries become very angry • Adversaries conspire to attack Jerusalem and create confusion • Adversaries decide to disguise themselves, dwell among the people, kill them and stop the work.	Sanballat (Horonite) (Tobiah) Ammonite, Geshem (Arabian), Army of Samaria, Ashdodites	Nehemiah 4:7-8, 11

THE VISION OF SUCCESS (NEHEMIAH'S VISION)

5	The wall is now built; there are no breaks in it. The vision implementation is almost complete.	• Adversaries focus their attention on leadership, try to seek audience from leadership multiple times, devise lies against leadership, try to bring spiritual underpinning to their lies, and tarnish the image of the leaders • Adversaries try to intimidate the leaders and put fear into them	Sanballat (Horonite), (Tobiah) Ammonite, Geshem (Arabian), Army of Samaria, Ashdodites	Nehemiah 6:1-8

| 6 | The gates are now built and installed; safety and security are restored. The work is complete. | • Try to intimidate the leaders, the true nature of the problem is revealed, a spiritual problem.
• Adversaries try to present a fake spiritual solution, employ the services of people who may pretend to be spiritual, try to make leadership afraid in order to abandon the vision.
• Adversaries become very disheartened in their own eyes.
• Adversaries acknowledge that the hand of God implemented the vision. | Sanballat (Horonite), (Tobiah) Ammonite, Geshem (Arabian), Army of Samaria, Ashdodites, fake men/women of God, fake prophets, fake prophetess | Nehemiah 6:10-13, 16 |
| 7 | The work is complete. Porters, singers, and Levites are appointed. Here the vision is fully implemented. | • Adversaries have been overpowered and defeated | All the enemies | Nehemiah 7: 1 |

- **3.5.1 EXTERNAL OPPOSITION:** This is an individual or group of people outside an organization or the vision-bearers' inner circle whose actions are antagonistic to the vision. External opposition is real and prevalent in most visions. There are indeed those who devise antagonistic plans and strategies to thwart the achievement of the vision. The goals of opposition are counterproductive and therefore the activities of such people will need to be monitored if one desires to succeed. Ignoring such people or individuals can be very detrimental to the vision. It is said that you have not yet succeeded until you have prevailed over the works of opposition. Sanballat, Tobiah, and their counterparts manifested as external opposition when they executed all the plans to destroy any possible progress of Nehemiah's vision.

What should I do?

The effect of external opposition must be managed; however, when it transitions to internal opposition, its danger and probability of success increases. The success rate increases because the internal oppositions may have access to more relevant information that may be employed against any potential progress.

> **3.5.2. INTERNAL OPPOSITION:** Internal opposition are a group of antagonistic people or individuals within an organization or within the inner circle of a vision-bearer. Usually these people are close to the source of the vision and may have access to secrets that may seriously impact the success of the vision. The works of internal opposition can be very dangerous. These people have access to more important information and can successfully be used against the works of the vision-bearers. The betrayal of Jesus by Judas Iscariot is an example of the level of success an internal opposition can achieve. As an Apostle of Jesus Christ, Judas Iscariot had access to vital information including His identity and schedule, which He used to betray Jesus Christ.

What should I do?

To be successful in every endeavor, one needs to be mindful of the existence of internal opposition. Sometimes, these people disguise themselves as supporters of the vision but on the contrary, they seek to destroy any possible success. In Chapter 6 of the book of Nehemiah, the opposition of Sanballat and his crew metamorphosed from external to internal. They hired people like Shemaiah as internal operatives against the work of rebuilding the walls of Jerusalem.

Always be mindful of the internal opposition who may seem to be supporting the vision but their true intentions are otherwise. Many people have had the shock of their lives by discovering the true opposition against their visions. Sometimes, out of jealousy or sheer wickedness, close confidants may be the force against the implementation of a vision. Nehemiah truly identified these people and denied them the level of access or influence they were seeking. Church leaders, political parties, business institutions, and other organizations must be mindful of internal oppositions by ensuring that such people do not have access to the inner information or position of influence that can be leveraged against the vision.

3.5.3 SPIRITUAL OPPOSITION (NEHEMIAH 6:10-14 NKJV)

We live in a world where the physical is controlled by the spiritual. Any physical occurrence is a manifestation of spiritual establishment. Success must therefore be established in the spiritual world before it is manifested in the physical. The spiritual battles that most visions have to engage in before they become successful stories are not something to downplay.

In the reading above, we realized how the spiritual opposition

THE VISION OF SUCCESS (NEHEMIAH'S VISION)

played out. Shemaiah presented a proposal that seemed a spiritual solution to Nehemiah; subsequently, Prophet Noadiah and other prophets employed spiritual intimidation tactics to thwart the work of God. However, through discernment, Nehemiah identified the spirit behind Shemaiah, Prophet Noadiah, and the other false prophets.

In the case of Nehemiah, there was a physical manifestation of spiritual warfare, but not all spiritual warfare will have a physical manifestation.. Most people will need to battle their visions through the realm of the spirit before they can become a success story. Whatever vision you carry, know that it must be established in the spiritual realm first.

The enemy is always against the seed of the righteous (Revelation 12:4 NIV), for we wrestle not against flesh and blood (Ephesians 6:12 NIV). If you are travailing to birth your vision, or there seems to be a strong delay and opposition against the manifestation of your vision, remember that not all oppositions are physical, so take the battle to the spiritual realms (2 Corinthians 10:4 NKJV) and I can assure you that a spiritual win will guarantee a physical success. Destroy the spiritual opposition and you will prevail in the physical. (For more information on spiritual warfare, read my book *The Weapons of our Warfare*,)

"Every success story is the cumulative result of a well-planned and executed series of tasks and activities."

4. PLANNING (PROVERBS 16:1, 9 NKJV) NEHEMIAH 2: 12-17 NIV)

Successes do not just occur. Every success story is the cumulative result of a well-planned and executed series of tasks and activities. Wishful thinking does not produce a successful outcome, neither does hoping. Planning is an essential personal or business tool that provides direction towards the achievement of vision, goals, or objectives. Whether you are seeking to start or improve upon a business, career, family, ministry, school, or write a book, planning will increase your chances of success tremendously. Planning helps you break your vision into smaller achievable pieces (see the Vision Map), reveals the strengths and weaknesses of a vision, and reduces risks and possibility of failure. It also increases efficiency, certainty, credibility, creativity and confidence, improves decision-making, and enhances the prospect of success.

Planning is the time spent to fully access the vision, derive alternative paths of implementation, and undertake a detailed analysis to increase the chances of success. Time spent in planning is as productive as the time spent in execution. Abraham Lincoln is noted to have said, "Give me six hours to chop down a tree and I will spend the first four sharpening the axe." The first four hours is the time for planning. Once proper planning is put in place, execution becomes easier. Sometimes people have a misconception that planning is time wasting because they do not see a direct output from such activities. However, this is a misconception, because per the analogy of Abraham Lincoln, once the axe is sharp, cutting down the tree becomes much easier and quicker.

Nehemiah's Plan

One of the greatest success characteristics exhibited by Nehemiah was his ability to plan. After hearing the news and spending time in fasting and prayer, he resorted to planning. From the scriptures, it is evident that he planned for his trip back to Jerusalem. He knew when he was going to leave and return, the items that would be needed for the trip, the raw materials, and the person responsible for those raw materials. Eventually when Nehemiah got to Jerusalem, he took some time to inspect the work, after which he planned for the implementation (Nehemiah 2:11-15 NKJV). His plan included all the parts of the broken walls that needed to be fixed, the group/individual responsible for each piece, the gates that needed repairs, the sequence of events, and many more. No wonder the work was completed in less than two months. Such a remarkable achievement could not have happened by chance; it occurred through a well thought out and executed plan.

God had a plan for creation, redemption, and various plans for the world and humanity. There is nothing sinful or unholy about planning one's life. Holy Spirit-baptized believers must understand that planning their lives is biblical and spiritual; in fact, the Holy Spirit works with a plan. Plan your spiritual growth, your ministerial path, your career or academic life, your marital and family life. Planning is a sure way to success. When our plan aligns with the counsel or the purpose of Jehovah, the intent of such plan shall stand (Proverbs 19:21 NIV) and its execution will glorify the name of the Lord.

A life plan serves as a road map for accomplishing what really matters. Once you know where you are and where you are going, you are in a position to create an action plan for getting there. A life plan should not be complicated, but must be easy to understand, with well-defined milestones.

5. PERSISTENCE
(LUKE 18, LUKE 11, NEHEMIAH 6:3 NIV)

Another orbit of success displayed by Nehemiah and his team was their persistence even in the midst of deadly opposition. Persistence has multiple dimensions to its meaning and may include the act of continuity amidst challenges, the existence for a prolonged period, and progression without interruption. The impact of persistence is implied by Jim Watkins' statement, "A river cuts through rock, not because of its power, but because of its persistence."

Persistence is defined as "voluntary continuation of a goal-directed action in spite of obstacles, difficulties, or discouragement" (Peterson and Seligman, 2004, p. 229). In relation to vision, I define persistence as the ability to continuously channel obstacle-surmounting effort towards a visualized future state and to transition from imagination into a reality. Persistence is born out of confidence, determination, fearlessness, and adaptability. No matter the level of opposition or obstacle, persistence pays off over time and can be very rewarding.

Nehemiah was very persistent in his vision pursuit and did not allow any obstruction to derail his pursuit even though there were many of them. In Luke chapter 11, Jesus taught His disciples how to pray, but this teaching expanded beyond words. This teaching also exposed the right attitude for impactful and successful prayers. One of the attitudes alluded to in Jesus' teachings was the quality of persistence. Jesus recounted an unpleasant scenario where a request was made at the wrong time and met a response of denial. However, because of the persistence in the request, the denial decision was rescinded and the demand granted. The great lesson is that no matter what, how, where, who and on whom a demand is placed, the power of persistence will yield the right results.

Ultimately, success is the ability to achieve the intended or expected results. Although some paths to success may be seen as relatively easier than others, most paths to success can be very challenging, and the power of persistence is needed to face and overcome the potential challenge.

Whether you are undertaking some form of business, ministry, politics, academics, or any aspect of life decision, your ability to persist will determine your ability to succeed. Persistence is not giving up even when all odds are against you, not resting your laurels when achievement seems not to have been attained, or not letting the numerous obstacles of life prevent you from attaining your vision and mission. To persist in vision pursuit is to channel your energy, effort, aspiration, desires, passion, and your whole being towards a common focal point called the vision. The focus must be consistent over time to ensure the realization and achievement of success.

Demonstration of Persistent Focus

During my elementary school days, there was a common science experiment where students used magnifying lenses to harvest sunlight over a large area and focus the sunrays on a pile of dry leaves or paper over time to spark fire. We were all amazed at the remarkable results the first time this experiment was conducted. The magnifying lens acts by bending the rays of light and focusing them, which results in intensifying the energy from a collection of all the rays to a focal point. Persistence for success should be viewed within the same context, by focusing all your energy towards a common task, project or vision. Over time, the intensity of the energy becomes so strong it will consume any obstacle or opposition to your success. Remember, the goal is to maintain focus over an extended period.

Exhortation

I want to encourage any vision-bearer reading this book to persevere in your vision pursuit. Yes, sometimes it can be difficult, discouraging, gloomy, fearful, and feel hopeless but the spirit of persistence and perseverance will always cause you to prevail. If you persist in your focus on the vision and give yourself time, you will succeed. Whatever your vision is, your persistence is a sure way of ensuring your arrival at the destiny of success. If you have abandoned your vision, go back for it and persistently pursue it, and you will surely arrive successfully. No matter how little advancement you make, if you do not turn to the left or to the right, such advancement will build upon itself and will eventually take you to the land of success. So keep on pushing and moving!

6. PATIENCE

The sixth orbit of success is to exercise patience, which is defined as the capacity to accept or tolerate delay, trouble, or suffering without getting angry or upset. It is said that patience can move mountains. Exercising patience is bitter but its fruit is sweet. Patience is essential for achieving any vision in life. This is because there is always a time gap between conception and realization of vision. Depending on the type of vision, the time gap can last from days to years. This calls for amassing the effect of patience and perseverance, especially where the phases of the vision last for many years. The synergistic effect between patience and perseverance can be magical and may cause every difficulty or obstacle to be subdued. Thus, patience is not only the ability to wait, but also being calm no matter what happens, constantly taking action to turn negative situations into positive growth opportunities, and having assured expectation and solid belief that the projected outcome will be achieved. Such patience is mostly anchored on faith, and without it many may throw in the towel when vision seems to have been delayed or when their achievement seems to be elusive.

Patience in a Fast-Paced World

We live in a fast-paced world, where instant gratification is the backdrop of many decisions. Many would rather eat and drink on the go. One may virtually travel to multiple countries within a minute and may be engaged in multiple tasks at the same time. This type of environment has deprived many of the virtue of patience. Many people have lost their ability to wait for achievement or results. Therefore, it is becoming increasingly difficult for some people to allocate the right amount of time for their vision to transcend through its phases and properly mature before its realization. Some may conceive a vision today and expect its realization tomorrow. Such expectations are not realistic. Note that every good vision must go through multiple phases for growth and development before realization. Without patience, any ounce of delay may be perceived as a sign of failure.

Sometimes, I imagine how long it took Noah to build an ark big enough to accommodate his family and two of every living thing on earth (Genesis 6:19 NKJV). In addition to that, let's think of the level of patience he needed to exercise to allow some of the slowest animals in the world like the sloth, snail, and tortoise to travel into the ark. Patience is a virtue, and its presence is important to tolerate delays, setbacks, and obstacles. Whatever your vision is, know that it will take time to bring it into reality. And while you wait actively, it is your level of patience that will determine your ability to transition through the phases and achieve the right level of success. Remember, Jesus waited for about 33 years to execute His salvation agenda on the cross, Abraham waited for about 25 years for the fulfillment of his covenant, and Moses was trained for 40 years before being handed the leadership mantle of Israel. Your time of waiting is not wasted.

7. PRIORITIZATION

Prioritization is the seventh orbit of success. This is because humanity is often bombarded with multiple options, and it takes prioritization to identify the options and assign appropriate ranking to facilitate the right decision-making.

Nehemiah exhibited a high sense of setting priorities in his judgment. As the cupbearer at the king's palace, Nehemiah had access to probably the finest wine, choicest food, and other provisions. He could have chosen to remain at the palace and enjoy all the choicest food. However, Nehemiah prioritized the task of going to help his people over staying in Persia and serving King Artarxexes. Even back in Jerusalem, he prioritized the welfare of the people over his personal comfort and provision. He also prioritized the work of rebuilding the walls of Jerusalem over his own safety and security. His ability to complete the work in less than two months was remarkable and partly due to prioritization.

Importance of Prioritization

Prioritization is vital to building and maintaining focus, allocating resources and energy, staying productive and reducing stress, and ensuring productivity and progress. Due to the possibility of competing options and alternatives, those who do not prioritize will become jacks-of-all-trades and masters of none. Prioritization helps one to learn to say no to tasks that are not important or do not align with your vision or objective. Through the process of prioritization, all options or tasks are identified and each of them is branded whether they are must, should, can, or desired to have.

THE VISION OF SUCCESS (NEHEMIAH'S VISION)

Success-bound and visionaries learn how to prioritize their tasks to avoid the possibility of chasing after their own tails. Such identified options are ranked based on their indispensability. Below are some steps for setting priorities.

1.1 Identify and List Tasks: Create a list of all your tasks or possible options

1.2 Identify What is Important: Based on the contribution or relevance of the tasks towards the achievement of the vision or goal. High priority tasks are those that are indispensable or urgently needed for the fulfillment of the vision.

1.3 Rank the Tasks: Rank the tasks based on the priority from the highest to the lowest. High priority tasks are given high numbers and those remaining reduced numbers according to their level of importance.

1.4 Identify and Avoid Competing Options: Identify all competing options and eliminate the lowest prioritized and competing tasks. Minimize or eliminate any possible distraction.

1.5 Schedule Priorities: Channel your energy, time, and resources towards implementation based on the rank of priority. Through this, allocated energy, time and resources are appropriately channeled to ensure the optimal utilization of these resources.

1.6 Risk Assessment and Evaluation: Risk assessment must be a continuous process throughout the implementation of the vision. This is because changes in task execution and environment may trigger change in the potential impact of risk. Execution and change in environment may also cause the birth of another risk. Continuously assessing the potential risks and evaluating their impact will help identify risk mitigation strategy. Prioritization helps in risk identification, assessment, and evaluation. Through this process, high-risk tasks are replaced with lower-risk tasks.

The idea behind prioritization is an acknowledgement that you cannot achieve everything you desire to accomplish in life. Time is a limited resource and must be apportioned appropriately. Without setting priorities, one may be very busy and engaging but may achieve very little or nothing.

8. PURPOSE

"Your purpose is what you were created to accomplish, the very reason for your existence."

True success can be defined, achieved, sustained, and measured within the scope of purpose. Your purpose is what you were created to accomplish, the very reason for your existence. Therefore, you are truly successful when your achievements aligns with your purpose. There is a specific reason behind every invention, production, or creation. To know the reason, one must humbly consult the inventor, producer, or creator. In the same way, there is that particular reason behind the creation of every person. Irrespective of the circumstance under which your creation manifested, there is a specific reason for your existence and that is the scope by which your success should be measured. Therefore, success is not solely based on the magnitude of achievement or accomplishment, but the extent to which those accomplishments align with and fulfill one's purpose.

Many people have made great strides and achieved enviable feats outside their purpose. Such people cannot be classified as successful because their accomplishments are devoid of their purpose. The magnitude of fulfillment one experiences for living a life in line with their God-given purpose is beyond description.

Purpose Applied

In our reference scripture, we realized that Nehemiah had achieved great feats even in a foreign land. He was a cupbearer in the king's palace and by default had access to the finest wine and by extension, access to assorted foods in the palace. However, Nehemiah did not assume a state of comfortability irrespective of the provisions he could access in the palace. Rather, he chose to return to the land of his birth, live among his people and lead them to restore their safety and security. As long as he stayed at the palace, his divine mandate was not to be fulfilled and success eluded him. However, when he realized that his mandate was not ordained at the palace, he accepted the call to depart to the broken city. That was a call to fulfill his purpose.

For many people, the place to achieve their divine mandate and fulfill their purpose is not in the palaces but the broken places, unattractive, vulnerable, hopeless, and rejected assignments. Some teachers are being called to the rejected countryside to educate hopeless children and turn their lives around. Entrepreneurs are being called to venture into unknown and less fancy businesses to experience their success. Ministers are being called to share the gospel in dangerous lands to save endangered souls from perishing. Others are being called to relocate to unattractive places where their success may be found. Whatever your vision is, seek to align it with your purpose. Your success and fulfillment will be beyond your wildest dream.

9. POTENTIAL

The ninth orbit of success evolves from potential. Potential is having or showing the capacity to become or develop into something in the future. A story is told of a pregnant woman carrying two boys in her womb. The struggle of the fetuses made her very uncomfortable; therefore, she decided to consult the Lord for the cause of the struggle in her womb. The Lord told her "two nations are in your womb." (Genesis 25:22-23 NIV) The question is how can two nations be in a womb? Nevertheless, the answer must be seen from the perspective of the vision, their future state and not the current. The seed of an oak tree may be seen as just a seed but has the potential of becoming a whole forest. Everyone has the potential of becoming someone greater, more powerful, influential, and successful beyond his or her wildest imagination. Therefore, when the Lord answered the woman that she was carrying two nations, the Lord was just unveiling to her the potential she was carrying.

You Carry Unlimited Potential

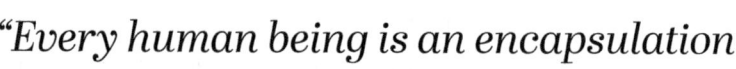

"Every human being is an encapsulation of unlimited potential!"

Every human being is an encapsulation of unlimited potential, which may be expressed through his or her knowledge, skills, and experiences. This unlimited potential can only be realized when we are located in a conducive environment and make decisions that will drive out the capabilities. Unfortunately, many people only realize a tiny percentage of their potential while others take almost their full potential to their graves. The environment we reside in (this includes the kind of company and friendships we keep), the way we think, act, and feel contribute towards the outcome of our potential. Although the impact of a single decision may be perceived as inconsequential, the cumulative effect over time will determine the level of growth, development, and realization of our potential. It is therefore possible to grow to a state of full potential, which is the optimal manifestation of one's capacity. Success is determined by the level and extent of manifestation of one's potential.

Sometimes, people do not attain success or achieve their vision because of dormant potential, fears, failure to act, or acting in an unconducive environment. Anyone who desires to achieve success must first identify and acknowledge the level of potential they carry and believe and activate their potential towards their vision. A dormant potential is as useless as no potential. Unfortunately, the potential of many people is lying in a state of dormancy waiting for either the right environment or some external force to trigger its activation. Dormant potentials are like seeds in the soil during the dry season. Though such seeds may stay in the soil without germinating, as soon as the rains come to create the right environment, they begin to shoot out.

The Biblical Application

Let us look at the story of Nehemiah's success. It is revealed that the inhabitants of the land executed the greater percentage of the work of rebuilding the walls and gates of Jerusalem. Nehemiah did not bring external labor to do the work, but rather he mobilized the labor force of the inhabitants. The people had great dormant potential that needed an external trigger to activate to execute the work. Nehemiah was that external force who came to activate, mobilize, channel their potential, and create the conducive environment for their operation. Thus, the enviable success story of Nehemiah hinges on the use of existing potential.

No matter how challenging your dreams, visions, goals, and aspirations, it is important to know that you already have the potential to succeed. Your success will depend on your ability to unveil the potential within you. To attain your full potential, you must develop a growth mindset, integrate reflection and action towards your vision, and appreciate the small steps that accumulate to the attainment of success. You have the potential; see yourself as an embodiment of success and take your rightful position.

10. PASSION (NEHEMIAH 4:6, ECCLESIASTES 9:10)

Passion is a strong, barely controllable emotion exerted towards someone, entity, or something. The foundation of every passion is desire. Desire is the seed of every great accomplishment. "To succeed, we must have a desire so strong that it reaches and permeates our subconscious minds." (Kazuo Inamori, 1995) If you have a desire to make a difference, the desire must grow and blossom to become a tree of passion. You must have passion for what you do to be successful in it. Passion is an intrinsic drive that propels you towards your vision, goal, or objective and it is essential for perseverance and persistence. Mostly, success is hard to achieve; therefore, without passion one will quit when difficulty is encountered. Without passion any rational person will give up when they encounter challenges; this is the reason why rationalism does not promote success. Develop passion for something, love what you do, and let your passion fuel you to success.

THE VISION OF SUCCESS (NEHEMIAH'S VISION)

"Develop passion for something and let your passion fuel you to success."

Biblical Application

There is clear evidence that Nehemiah approached this work with much passion. His passion was so strong and his vision so crystal clear that they became integrated into his subconscious mind and inseparable from his being. Upon receipt of the news of the vulnerable state of Jerusalem, he resorted to fasting and prayers and the passion within him exerted towards the project of restoration was evidenced in the change of his countenance (Nehemiah 2:2 NIV). He could not hide his displeasure and the issue that was brooding inside him. Even the king realized that not everything was all right. His passion was so embedded in the vision and infectious that all the workers became affected. He testified that the people worked with all their hearts (Nehemiah 4:6 NIV). Their passion towards the work was so strong that it elevated their commitment and subdued the possible intimidation from the camp of their enemies. They may have given up if they considered the magnitude of the threats, opposition, and intimidation they encountered during the rebuilding exercise. Nevertheless, the passion had possessed the people to the extent that there was absolutely no room for fear or intimidation. Being passionate about our work is highly Biblical (Ecclesiastes 9:10 NKJV). The Bible encourages us that whatever our hands find to do, we should do it with all our might. That is an encouragement to exert passion towards our undertaking.

The Success Formula

In his book entitled *A Passion for Success*, Kazuo Inamori indicated, "Without effort, a great vision will remain just an unfulfilled dream. No worthwhile goal has ever been attained without strenuous, meaningful labor." The journey to success is labor intensive and is propelled and sustained by a tailwind of passion. Kazuo Inamori's formula for success is expressed as Success = Ability X Effort X Attitude. He stated, "The degree of effort you expend in life depends upon your strong desire." Strong desire is "Passion" (Inamori, 1995); therefore, the degree of effort exerted towards your vision is directly proportional to your passion. Our success story is a product of our ability, effort, and attitude. No matter how talented you are (ability), without the proper amount of effort (underpinned by passion) and attitude, your success story may be mediocre or unrealized. The value of attitude assigned in the formula above ranges from -100 to +100. This means that a negative "success" may be achieved when a remarkable ability coupled with a great effort is exerted under a negative attitude. However, my focus here is the remarkable impact our passion can exert on our success story. Our knowledge, skill, and talent must be commensurate with great effort under a powerfully positive attitude for success to be realized.

	VISION HUMAN INTERACTION	
NO	**HUMAN ENTITY**	**DEFINITION AND INTERACTION**
1	The Visionary	• This person conceives the vision. • He is the brain, owner, inspiration, and driver of the vision. • Largely, the success or failure of the vision depends on him. • He must be the anchor throughout all the phases and the implementation process • Removal, elimination, or sidelining the visionary during execution exponentially increases the probability of failure. (Read Steve Job and Apple)

2	Those in Authority/Supervisors	• These are the people with authority over the visionary • Obtaining the favor and approval of this group/individual is essential and highly recommended in most cases. • Their approval may open other doors for access, support, or provision for the vision. • Sometimes these people may help in guiding the visionary to navigate through uncertain terrain. • They may also help in minimizing or eliminating the impact of opposition.
3	Vision Partners	• These are usually the early adaptors or supporters of the vision. • They catch the vision at the conception phase, align with the visionary, and provide diverse engagement or support towards the realization of the vision. • Sometimes they are the heralds or early propagators of the vision, especially within corporate settings. • Vision partners are dependable and seek for the success of the vision. • It is important for every visionary to properly identify their vision partners and provide opportunity for their involvement.
4	Vision Beneficiaries	• They are those who benefit either directly or indirectly from the successful implementation of the vision. • In the corporate world, they can be the shareholders, employees, or customers • In instances where the implementation of the vision leads to the provision of service or product, seeking the input or opinion of the beneficiaries can be beneficial. • Any possible solution derived from the implementation of vision must meet the needs of this group

5	Vision Opposition	<ul><li>They are those who do not seek for the successful realization of the vision.</li><li>Most visions may encounter some kind of opposition one way or another.</li><li>Sometimes they exert a certain level of effort against the vision.</li><li>Opposition could arise from either competitors or comrades.</li><li>Triggers of opposition include misunderstanding of vision, miscommunication, envy, defending ones' interest, or just an evil heart.</li><li>Opposition may be categorized as internal, external, or spiritual.</li></ul>

Chapter Summary

- Definition of Success: Success is a measure of cumulative achievements and engagements over a period. This includes engagements that did not yield the expected results. Success is predictable and the predictability factors include the rules of engagement with the ten orbits of success as listed below.

- The following are the ten orbits (10 "Ps") of success:

  - Problem: The first rule to success is identification of problem(s) and provision of solution. Problems are potential seeds to success and therefore, having the affinity to confront problems and the courage to overcome them are the foundation upon which the edifice of success stands.

  - Prayer: Prayer is the humanity and divinity interaction that opens the doors to the rooms of success.

  - People: The third rule of success is the identification of the people. There is no success story devoid of people; humanity is the centerpiece of every success story. Every vision may interact with the following five categories of people.

    - Visionaries: The first person to conceive the vision is called the visionary. He becomes the brain, direction, inspiration, and driver for the successful manifestation of the vision. The realization of most visions is elusive without the visionary.

    - People in Authority: This is the category of people who have authority over the visionary. Mostly their acceptance, decisions, and guidance can be very influential to the success of the visions. They must be treated with respect, honor, and tact with the ultimate goal of seeking their favor.

- Vision Partners: Vision partners are usually the early believers, supporters, advisors who seek to promote the achievement of the vision. They are the heralds who may run with the vision. Providing opportunity for these groups is essential to facilitate, lessen the load, and sometimes speed up the phases of the vision.

- Vision Beneficiaries: Those who derive either direct or indirect benefit from the implementation and execution of the vision. Mostly, seeking their input towards the manifestation of the vision is vital towards its success.

- Vision Opposition: Every vision has its opposition. These are the people who seek to counter, impede, or thwart the success of the vision. These people do not take delight in the realization of a vision and must therefore be denied access to any relevant information. Vision opposition can be categorized into three groups as indicated below.

  - External Opposition

  - Internal Opposition

  - Spiritual Opposition

- Planning: Success does not just occur; it must be planned and worked into existence. Every success story is the cumulative result of a well-planned and executed series of tasks and activities.

- Persistence: Persistence is the ability to continuously channel obstacle-surmounting effort towards a visualized future state. Persistence is born out of confidence, determination, fearlessness, and adaptability and it is a very essential sphere of every success story.

- Patience: The common adage that Rome was not built in a day is true guidance for those who seek success in every area of their lives. Patience is the ability to accept or tolerate what may seem delays or suffering without getting angry. Due to the default time differential between the time of conception and implementation, exercising patience is a required virtue to guarantee success.

- Priority: Prioritization is the ability to assign the right level of importance to competing tasks or alternatives and pursue such options based on the rank level of importance. Humanity is often bombarded with multiple options, and it takes prioritization to identify the options and assign the appropriate ranking to facilitate decision-making. Prioritization includes identifying and listing tasks, ranking and scheduling tasks based on importance, and identifying and avoiding competing options.

- Purpose: True success is defined, achieved, sustained, and measured within the scope of purpose. Purpose is the reason for creation and existence; therefore, purpose-aligned engagements and achievements are the ultimate indicators of success. The level of fulfillment experience encountered from the identification of one's purpose and achievement of purpose driven vision is simply indescribable and extremely gratifying.

- Potential: Potential is having or showing the capacity to become or develop into something or someone in the future. It is often understood from the perspective of value addition or attainment of a higher dimension of status. Every human being is an encapsulation of an unlimited potential; however, such potential needs to be located in a conducive environment and unveiled through appropriate decisions for it to be realized. Every potential has the capacity to become dormant if not well developed. Success is realized upon the activation and utilization of potential for an intended result.

- Passion: Passion is a strong, barely controllable emotion exerted towards someone, an entity, or something. Desire is the seed that must germinate, grow, and blossom to become a tree of passion. Passion generates an intrinsic drive that propels the visionary towards the pursuit of the vision, goal, or objective and is vital for perseverance and persistence. Without passion, any rational person may give up when they encounter challenges. This is why rationalism without passion does not promote success.

- Conclusion: The ten aforementioned orbits of success define the paradigm of success and apply the right ability, attitude, and effort to hold the centerpiece. They produce a guaranteed outcome of success in any dimension of life when well implemented.

CHAPTER FOURTEEN

THE VISION OF LEADERSHIP

(JETHRO-MOSES LEADERSHIP VISION)

(A leader's job is to look into the future and see the organization, not as it is, but as it should be. - Jack Welch)

> *"The vision of the evenings and mornings that has been given you is true, but seal up the vision, for it concerns the distant future."*
>
> **Daniel 8:26 NIV**

VISION STORY - JOHN MAXWELL

John Maxwell, born 1946, is a globally acclaimed author, leadership expert, speaker, coach, and pastor. In 2014, he was nominated by the American Management Association as the number one most influential leader in business. He has developed the five levels of leadership, which explains how a leader should perform to attain influence, respect, and success. His vision and passion for growing and equipping others to do remarkable things and lead significant and fulfilled lives has led him to author over two hundred books which have sold more than 35 million copies. From humble beginnings as a pastor leading several churches in the 1970s, it is his vision on leadership development that has propelled him as the de facto leader in global leadership development.

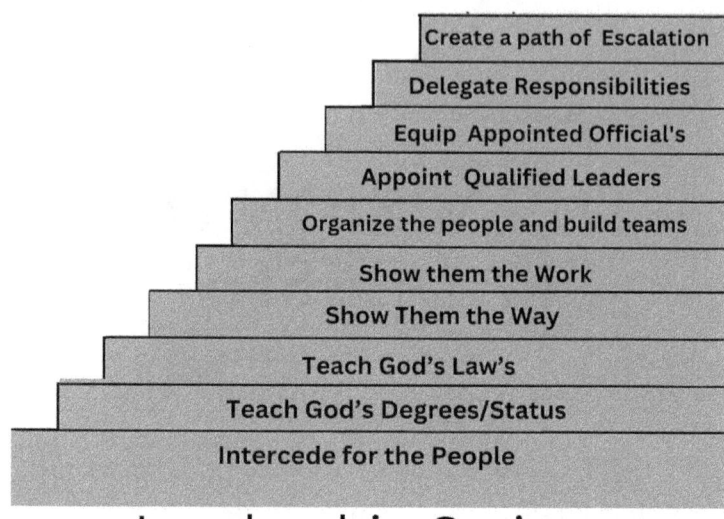

Leadership Stairs

INTRODUCTION

One of the most powerful and influential leadership counsels recorded in the Bible was given to Moses by his father-in-law, Jethro. After receiving an "Ivy League" education in an array of courses, including Egyptian civilization, politics, commerce, finance etc., at the Pharaoh's palace, Moses fell short in the proper execution of his leadership duties during the exodus of the Israelites from Egypt to the Promised Land. A careful study of Exodus 18:13-26 sets the tone for analyzing Moses-Jethro's leadership vision. With many years of priestly experience, Jethro had developed great universal leadership skills applicable to any area of life and transcending everything. The recommendations and strategies espoused in this part of scripture can be adopted and successfully applied to every sphere of leadership. I have termed these strategies as leadership vision, but first let us review the scripture for understanding and to gain insight .

> The next day Moses took his seat to serve as a judge for the people, and they stood around him from morning till evening. When his father-in-law saw all that Moses was doing for the people, he said, "What is this you are doing for the people? Why do you alone sit as a judge while all these people stand around you from morning till evening?"

> Moses answered him, "Because the people come to me to seek God's will. Whenever they have a dispute, it is brought to me, and I decide between the parties and inform them of God's decrees and instructions." Moses' father-in-law replied, "What you are doing is not good. You and these people who come to you will only wear yourselves out. The work is too heavy for you; you cannot handle it alone. Listen now to me, and I will give you some advice, and may God be with you. You must be the people's representative before God and bring their disputes to him. Teach them his decrees and instructions, and show them the way they are to live and how they are to behave. But select capable men from all the people—men who fear God, trustworthy men who hate dishonest gain—and appoint them as officials over thousands, hundreds, fifties and tens. Have them serve as judges for the people at all times, but have them bring every difficult case to you; the simple cases they can decide themselves. That will make your load lighter because they will share it with you. If you do this and God so commands, you can stand the strain, and all these people will go home satisfied.

> Moses listened to his father-in-law and did everything he said. He chose capable men from all of Israel and made

them leaders of the people, officials over thousands, hundreds, fifties, and tens. They served as judges for the people at all times. The difficult cases they brought to Moses, but the simple ones they decided themselves. (Exodus 18:13-26 NIV)

After hearing of God's spectacular rescue of the Israelites from Egypt, Jethro, the priest of Midian and Moses' father-in-law, embarked on a visitation to Moses and the Israelites with Moses' wife and two sons. Jethro's expected arrival to the camp of the Israelites was highly ceremonial. After exchanging pleasantries, they retired to the tent where Moses recounted everything the Lord had done to Pharaoh and the Egyptians for Israel's sake.

Jethro received the news with much delight; however, the following day, the blatant leadership flaws exhibited by his son-in-law took him aback. Moses' lack of good judgment, empathy, and delegation caused many of the Israelites who had social issues to return home after standing in a queue all day without their needs being met. He had taken the responsibility of judging all the people upon himself, resulting in dissatisfaction and exhaustion for both the people and himself. The manifestation of leadership flaws had impeded the progress to the Promised Land and their social health. Therefore, let us concentrate on the effective leadership counsel provided by Jethro. Jethro recommended ten (10) leadership strategies worth exploring, establishing, and maintaining. These success-bound strategies are effectively applicable to every leadership position and guarantee great results when properly applied. Let us journey through these strategies and see how they can be related and applied to God's business.

JETHRO-MOSES LEADERSHIP VISION STRATEGIES

1. INTERCEDE FOR THE PEOPLE

The first dimension of great leadership within the context of Christianity is to be an intercessor. Jethro's first recommendation was for Moses to represent the people before God. This meant that Moses should intercede for his people, standing before God and bringing their needs, challenges, and difficulties to God. His primary interest as a leader was to care for them, help them grow and develop their potential, and lessen their burdens. Since Moses could not rely on himself alone to complete this task, it was important for him to always be plugged into God for direction and guidance. In this way, Moses acknowledged his inadequacies and was able to submit himself to the total control of God in leading His people.

Spiritually empowered church leaders ought to be intercessors and seek the people's interests above theirs. This counsel from Jethro reveals the spiritual dimension of church leadership and the importance of maintaining spirituality in every leadership decision. Interceding for the people is the key to opening all the other doors in the lives of the people we lead.

THE VALOR OF VISION

"Spiritually empowered leaders ought to be intercessors and seek the people's interest above theirs."

One of the greatest success factors in leadership is the ability to represent the interest and meet the needs of the people. To properly accomplish this, a leader must seek to understand his followers by listening and paying attention to their needs. This strategy is applicable in every sphere or dimension of life. Throughout the world, great leading companies are those who have understood their markets and represent the interest of their customers through the provision of products and services that meet their needs. Such leading companies have attained this feat by paying attention to their customer base and presenting their interest as the highest agenda item during management and board meetings. Thus, the interest of the customers is presented at the highest level of organizational engagement and decision-making.

This same philosophy is true and applicable even in academia. The leading universities in every jurisdiction are those who present academic products or services that represent and meet the interest of the students and can be translated into value-added products and services in the marketplace. It is therefore not a coincidence that leading global universities have established a record of accomplishment of innovations or contributed significantly towards the marketplace of knowledge. Leaders, elected and appointed politicians, corporate executives, parents, and anyone holding leadership positions must understand that they are better and more impactful leaders if their decisions are made and executed against the backdrop of the needs, challenges, difficulties, issues, and problems of the people. Therefore, the advice of Jethro to Moses can be literally translated as when you meet God (the highest decision-making meeting) do not present your interest, but rather carry the interest of the people to this great spiritual board meeting. This is the first sign of manifesting great leadership skills in every area of life.

2. TEACH THEM GOD'S DECREES/STATUTES

Humans are social beings; we influence and are influenced by others. Our character development and behavior determinations are affected positively and negatively by these social dynamics. With this understanding, Jethro advised Moses to impart the knowledge needed to help the Israelites live with each other. In other words, Moses was to teach them how to live responsibly with each other and within the universe to create a productive and sustainable social environment. The decrees/statutes of God are meant to reveal God's plan, purpose, or intentions in governing the universe. By this, Moses was to develop a system, which would ensure the people established enforceable social rules and regulations. Understanding and implementing these decrees would invariably reduce the number of prevailing social issues. It was important for Moses to be proactive and not reactive. That is, instead of Moses waiting for problems to surface before sharing insight from God, he should rather make these insights known to the people. This understanding would help the Israelites know the acceptable way of living with each other. The decrees/statutes of God were to be their guidelines, policies, rules, regulations, and expectations. They were to shape their thought processes and character formation and assist in averting some of the numerous issues that were emanating from the camp. Understanding the statutes was essential to understanding God's expectations and fostering a better relationship between each other. Eventually, an acceptable social order was to be established through the teachings of the decrees of the Lord.

"Understanding makes everything easier."

Application

It is incumbent on every good leader to teach their people to understand how to live within their scope of operation. Parents must teach their children the proper social norms and standards. Corporate executives are to teach their workers to develop productive social lifestyles within the organization that will positively impact their coworkers and customers alike. Church leaders must not only teach on spirituality that leads to eternity, but on social lifestyles that will create a united and peaceful community of believers for the Holy Spirit to operate in.

The use of the word "teach" here must not be misconstrued as a lecture room type impartation of knowledge, but should rather be viewed within the lens of influencing and setting the right expectations for relationship building, communication, commitment, and establishing boundaries. Great leaders have mastered the skills of influencing their environment subtly. Such skills should be employed to create an organizational culture that adds value to their employees and reflects a continuous improvement in their products or services. Creating such an environment in homes, workplaces, or places of worship will establish and maintain individual or organizational leadership in their marketplace.

3. TEACH THEM GOD'S LAW (PSALM 78:5)

Moses was to teach them God's laws so they could understand how to relate to Him. The laws were rules and regulations that governed the relationship between Israel and their Creator. It was Moses' responsibility to help Israel understand that breaking any of the laws (sin) offended God and had consequences. Moreover, it separated and fractured their relationship with God, leading to the potential loss of their God-given benefits. Moses' successful completion of this task was dependent on his exemplary life, his adherence to those laws, and establishing a deeper and closer relationship with God. It is difficult for a spiritual leader to consistently teach others how to have a close relationship with God if he does not have one of his own. How can one teach if they do not practice what they teach? Yes, it is very possible to fake it, but doing such is depending on one's own strength, which has a limit. Eventually the truth will be revealed, and he will be naked and ashamed. As you, the leader, continue to pour into others, you must remember to fill your own cup. You have missed your ultimate objective and purpose of Christian leadership if you do not promote and foster a deeper connection between you and God and God and those you serve.

Application

Every nation, society, industry, profession, or business operates within and it is governed by relevant laws. The third rule of leadership is to know or employ the services of someone who knows the applicable laws pertaining to the areas of operation. To be a Christian leader, you must know the laws of God and apply them successfully, especially in this era of grace. Intentionally flaunting the laws of God under the pretense of grace will negate the provisions of God's grace. To be a leader in your industry or line of business, you must know and rightfully apply the laws. In short, one must know and correctly apply the laws of their area in order to become a leader in that field. Ignorance or inability to apply applicable laws in any field is definitely a recipe for failure and may expose you to certain avoidable risks.

Here again we see the need for pro-activeness in teaching the laws of God for the purpose of risk management. Laws pertaining to spiritual matters, corporate entities, national and international organizations, intellectual property, and many more are all enacted to set the framework for compliance and are essential prerequisites for leaders in their prospective fields. Knowledge of the laws that govern an area of operation is essential to establish leadership effectiveness. Individuals or organizations who apply this strategy have set themselves apart for significant leadership exploits and success.

4. SHOW THEM THE WAY

The fourth strategy for effective leadership establishment is to show your people the way. It is said that you cannot take people to a destination to which you are incapable of going. Jethro continued his counsel by asking Moses to show the Israelites the way. "Since they had the pillar of cloud and fire for their physical direction, this admonition must refer to showing them their life direction as a spiritual counselor." [6] Showing them the way meant Moses was to be an example for them, just as the Apostle Paul was to be for the Church in Corinth (1 Corinthians 11:1 NIV).

---

6 Ibid, 39

LEADERSHIP BY EXAMPLE

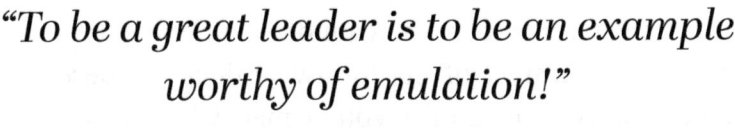

"To be a great leader is to be an example worthy of emulation!"

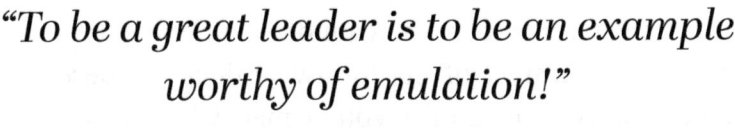

To be a great leader is to be an example worthy of emulation. Great leaders have followers because they are valuable products themselves or provide desirable services that impact the lives of their followers. To show them the way means to give them access to yourself, your decisions, and yourt thought processes. For example, a pastor whose character cannot be emulated by his congregation is only occupying a position but not leading. However, in certain areas of life, one's character does not serve as the standard for imitation. It is often said that kids do not do what they are told but what they see.

To show the way also means that you must be confident in taking followers to the intended destination based on your record of accomplishment. The great American investor, Warren Edward Buffett, and his company's (Berkshire Hathaway) investment decisions (stock purchases and portfolio composition) have been followed and imitated by millions of people in the investment field throughout the world. Berkshire Hathaway has provided consistently remarkable investment leadership for decades and has shown the way through their enviable return on investment. That is a typical case of showing the way or being a true example worthy of emulation.

Leadership is Sacrifice

Showing the way will sometimes mean the leader putting his/her life at risk or sacrificing their interest and safety for the sake of their followers. A leader who cannot assume risk or render sacrifice for the betterment of his followers does not deserve to be followed. A story is told of a young man who had three of his senior brothers enlisted in the national army and deployed on a battlefield to defend the nation. This young man was sent on an errand and upon arrival on the battlefield, he witnessed the display of the might and military prowess of their enemy. In addition to that, he was amazed by the absence of leadership exhibited by his national army. No one was ready to show the way. No one wanted to be an example, and no one wanted to take on the risk for the betterment of the nation. Lack of leadership was on full display, though many people were occupying various leadership positions. This young man showcased his leadership qualities by offering to take on the risk and sacrifice himself for the nation. He singlehandedly took down the leadership of the enemy's military, and subsequently championed an extraordinary massacre of their enemies. No wonder he became the de facto leader of his nation from that day (1 Samuel 17 NKJV).

Anyone aspiring to effective and efficient leadership must employ the strategy of showing the way to his or her followers. This way, your followers will develop confidence in you and aspire to follow your footsteps.

5. SHOW THEM THE WORK

The next strategic leadership counsel to Moses was to show the Israelites the work they were to perform. Showing them the work meant that Moses must communicate clearly and consistently their roles and responsibilities and help them appreciate their assignments. Roles and responsibilities are the tasks and functions every member of the team must perform to facilitate the reaching of common goals and objectives. Everyone ought to know, understand, and agree to their respective assignments within the organization. Achieving this feat is for multiple reasons, including: helping the members of the team align their efforts and resources to a common goal, vision, and strategy; harmonizing their actions, decisions and implementation within and among the members; avoiding duplication, overlaps, and potential gaps; building accountability and ownership, and eventually fostering cohesion and collaboration among members of the organization. Lack of or inadequate communication of roles and responsibilities within an organization creates confusion, frustration, and conflicts resulting in underperformance, negative morale, and lack of trust. If Moses was to become a great leader with assurance of taking the people to the Promised Land (the vision), then it was imperative that he master this art of communication.

Skill Development

Showing them the work also meant he needed to help them build the knowledge and develop essential success-bound skills. Building the prerequisite understanding to perform tasks and functions creates opportunity for performance improvement. A key success factor of efficient leadership is not only to assign the roles and responsibilities, but also to help or provide the necessary skills, tools, and environment conducive for performing those functions. Moses needed to train the people to know their work and either directly or indirectly help them perform their functions successfully. Thus, creating expertise is an important factor in efficient leadership execution.

Not One Man's Job

Showing them the work also meant Moses humbly accepted that he alone could not perform all the functions. Indeed, the work was too much for him alone; he could not execute everything by himself. Being a leader does not mean performing all the roles and responsibilities by yourself; every leader needs help. Therefore, identifying and selecting the right resources, training, and empowering people is an excellent recipe for leadership success. Moses needed to learn how to "duplicate himself" so that his other selves would contribute towards the execution of the various functions. Leadership is about reproducing your kind in terms of ability to perform the roles and responsibilities successfully.

This strategy of showing them the work as explained above is vital and applicable to every leadership position, including parenting, ministry, government, corporate, academia, and many more. Great and powerful leaders learn how to assign roles and responsibilities, help their followers understand exactly what and how to do their work, create self-improvement opportunities and capacity building techniques, and "reproduce" many of their kind. This way, members in the organization are intentionally set for success and gradually minimize their dependency on the overall leader.

Biblical Application

From Genesis 12, we understand that God intended to call the people of Israel His chosen nation and use them as a channel to facilitate His redemption of humanity. This work has not changed even though the criteria for becoming a member of God's family has broadened from being a Jew to believing in Jesus Christ (Romans 3:23-26, John 1:12; 1 Thessalonians 1:4; 2 Thessalonians 2:13-14; Galatians 3: 26-29). In order to ensure continuity and sustenance of legacies, which is one of the qualities of leadership, organizational leaders should learn how to pour themselves, prepare and equip others to equally lead and succeed.

6. APPOINT QUALIFIED LEADERS

The sixth strategy for leadership success is to always appoint, elect, or select qualified people to positions of authority. Moses was tasked to organize the people into manageable groups and appoint able leaders over them. This qualification for leadership was not based on family or tribal ties, physical appearance, or educational status but on competence (capable and strong), the fear of God (humility with understanding and appreciation for both divine and human fellowship), adherence to truth (trustworthy, honest), and rejection of covetousness (be above bribery and corruption, have integrity). All these internal qualities affect the mind and the heart and are needed to facilitate appropriate decision-making. This is because one of the fundamental responsibilities of leadership is decision-making and influence. A corrupt mind and heart will make corrupt decisions, influence their people with corruption, and produce corrupt followers. Any organization under the leadership of people with the aforementioned prescribed character traits is bound to succeed.

Leaders Must Be Led

An excellent leadership organizational structure is when every leader has a leader or reports to someone. This ensures that everyone is responsible for and accountable to someone. It is said that power corrupts; therefore, no individual or leader must have absolute power or authority in any organization. Even the most anointed, morally upright, and ethically sound leader must operate within suitable checks and balances and be accountable to someone. Against the backdrop of the recommendations above is a revelation that selection of leadership is a daunting task and must not be taken for granted in any capacity. Placing an unqualified person in any leadership position affects not only the organization and the leaders' performance negatively, but may also ripple through the lives of current and future generations or members. I therefore want to leave to your imagination the potential long-term detrimental impact of choosing an unqualified political leader into a national leadership position.

Leadership From Within

Again, Moses was tasked to choose qualified men from out of the people. This criterion is equally essential for leadership selection for any organization. Choosing from out of the people implies appointing those who share the common vision, goals, and aspirations of the organization. Those who understand and subscribe to the organization's vision are to be brought into leadership. For the purpose of organizational leadership selection strategy, this categorization may not necessarily mean only current members or employees but may also include prospective employees or members. The underlying factor is their subscription or aspiration of sharing the vision of the organization. Such people have a shorter or lower learning curve and are able to assume their positions quicker.

Every society, community, or nation is better off in the end if led by God-fearing men who prioritize competence and truth and hate covetousness. I want to encourage nations, political parties, churches, corporations, businesses, and families to adhere to this recommendation of choosing the right people for every leadership position. This will ensure progressive development and positive societal transformations.

7. ORGANIZE THE PEOPLE AND BUILD TEAMS

Another evidence of effective leadership is the ability to create workable groups or teams within an organization. It is said that teamwork makes the dream/vision work. The seventh strategy for Moses to develop efficiency in his leadership was to organize the people into groups and create manageable, workable, formidable, and productive teams. This is because any effective leader must develop the skill of leading both individuals and teams alike. Establishing a working team environment allows individual members to bring their diverse perspectives in problem solving which results in the development of an efficient and effective solution. Just as roles and responsibilities are better managed when divided into tasks, organizations are equally better managed through the formation of teams. Proper formation and cohesion in team effort may result in improved productivity, communication and creativity, development of better problem- solving skills, increased accountability, and reduced risk of exhaustion.

Why Team Building?

"Group synergy enhances productivity and performance."

Team building is an essential prerequisite for leadership development, and every effort should be channeled toward its implementation. Group synergy enhances productivity and performance when members of the team are cohesively and collaboratively executing their functions. Group synergies are well-demonstrated using relays as against individual running. The fastest 100-meter run of all time is 9.58 seconds and was achieved by Usain Bolt of Jamaica on August 16th, 2009. If four athletes with the same Usain Bolt speed were asked to run 100 X 4 meters, their fastest speed should be 38.32 seconds. However, due to synergistic effect, the world fastest 100 X 4 meters, completed by Nesta Carter, Michael Frater, Yohan Blake, and Usain Bolt, was achieved in 36.84 seconds, two seconds below the estimated time above. This saving is attributable to the synergy within the group. Indeed, the importance and benefits of group synergy cannot be overemphasized when there is enough cohesion between and among the members of the group. Great leaders are strategic in forming smooth functioning groups in their organizations.

Biblical Application

Moses was advised to build teams comprising groups of thousands, hundreds, fifties, and tens, with a leader over each group. The strategy was to start prospective leaders over the group of tens and subsequently promote them over groups of fifties, hundreds, and thousands as and when their competence allowed. With this strategy, anyone who did not exhibit competence by exerting positive influence over few would miss the opportunity of leading many. Organizational leadership ascension can rely on this strategy to develop competent leaders. Inability to execute required roles and responsibilities over few must stall any opportunity for further progression or ascension through the organizational leadership ladder. Every leader is welcome to implement this result-dependent leadership strategy in their various spheres of engagements.

8. EMPOWER APPOINTED OFFICIALS

Appointing officials over groups of thousands, hundreds, fifties, and tens was a remarkable leadership strategy, but such leaders must be equally empowered for effective execution of their duties. This empowerment could include being allocated the right level of authority, independence, knowledge, skills, and tools.

Moses was to empower them by assigning the right level of authority to enable such officials to administer justice effectively. These appointed officials were to judge the people at all times, and therefore it was important that they had the right level of authority to make appropriate decisions. Operating with authority at all times ensures that people's issues do not encounter unnecessary delays but receive prompt or immediate attention. Such an environment is necessary for the continuous management of cases and to ensure the possibility for de-escalation. It is important to emphasize that empowering officials and leaders is an effective way of setting leaders up for success. This is how burdens or responsibilities are shared. Unfortunately, some leaders may create positions and assign resources without empowering those resources to execute their duties effectively. Without the right level of authority, no leader can administer their work effectively and produce other leaders.

No Micro-Management

Empowering the officials is to grant them the right level of independence to function. Leaders work better when they are granted a level of autonomy to make their own decisions. Leadership confidence is boosted when they know that their leaders believe in them and trust their judgment. Great leaders eschew micro-management and micro-leadership. Micro-management is when the leader is involved in every level of the decision-making process. Such strategy does not produce confident leaders, hinders innovation and creativity, and may cause unnecessary delays in the execution of roles and responsibilities. Every good leader must learn how to empower others by providing a degree of independence in the performance of their duties. It is also important to strike a balance between supervision and autonomy. Finding the right level is vital for developing other leaders and leveraging diversity and creativity within the team.

Empowering officials is also to provide them the necessary knowledge, skills, and tools for executing their duties. People are empowered when they have access to the right level of knowledge, well developed skills, and operate with the appropriate tools. When Moses was asked to teach the Jewish followers, it was in fulfillment of providing the right knowledge. However, acquisition of knowledge alone is insufficient to ensure performance improvement. It is the proper application of knowledge that creates the recipe for improvement and success. Skill is the ability to apply knowledge to produce expected results. Skills are developed not only through acquisition of knowledge but also through experience. People are empowered when they are granted the opportunity to develop their skills by practicing their knowledge. Therefore, every proper leadership educational system must adhere to the principles of knowledge acquisition and skill development. This is one distinguishing hallmark between the educational system of most developed and underdeveloped countries. Empowering the people also meant that Moses must provide them the right tools for their work. This third dimension of empowerment is essential to raising other leaders and providing an efficient operational system within any organization.

Contrasting Worldview and Christian View of Empowerment

Spiritual empowerment is a vital form of empowerment for those who have spiritual awareness and are spiritually active. The worldview of spiritual empowerment hinges on self-discovery, awareness, and developing the power and freedom to explore your soul, beliefs, and identity. However, the Christian view of empowerment goes beyond self and rather anchors on reliance on God (the Holy Spirit) to provide capacity for spiritual engagement and exploits. To the Christian believer, our strength is not from ourselves but from a divine power who owns, controls, directs, and sanctions the execution of everything in the world. Christian empowerment is derived from our knowledge and rightful application of the Word of God, and other spiritual exercises such as fasting, prayer, and divine fellowship. Therefore, whereas provision of authority, the right level of autonomy, knowledge, skills, and tools meet worldview empowerment, Christian leaders must implement those in addition to the spiritual empowerment exercises listed above to be successful in the execution of their duties.

The call of Moses to empower the appointed officials meant to consider and implement all the aforementioned aspects of empowerment. This is because the journey from Egypt to the Promised Land did not only represent a physical relocation but also signified a spiritual repositioning. It was therefore important for leaders of such groups and teams to be equally empowered physically and spiritually, in order to meet the multi-dimensional needs of the people and their journey. Leaders of spiritual organizations must take note of this fact and empower their members appropriately.

9. DELEGATE RESPONSIBILITIES

Another strategy for leadership manifestation is the ability to delegate responsibility to other leaders or followers. Delegation of responsibility is the transfer of responsibility for specific tasks or roles from one person to another. For it to be effective, it is always necessary to accompany delegation of responsibility with the right level of authority. Effective delegation ensures optimum productivity in the organization and empowers team members to acquire new skills and develop innovative methods to attain the institutional or business visions and objectives. Delegation is not abandonment of functions; on the contrary, it must be accompanied by adequate supervision to ensure the proper execution of duties.

In Exodus 18:22, Jethro indicated, "the simple cases they can decide themselves." This called for Moses to delegate some of the responsibility to the officials or the judges after they have been empowered. On observing the trend of events right from the beginning till now, responsibilities are not to be delegated to people who have not been prepared and empowered. The empowered officials were to be responsible for deciding on the simple matters; the ones that did not require complex reasoning or in-depth understanding were to be handled by the judges. In this way, the judges would hold a more significant percentage of issues, releasing Moses to concentrate on the complex issues. In reference to the "simple cases," Tidwell explained, "these were the common kinds of problems which were covered by statutes and laws, or which were of limited magnitude. This kind of problem was to be solved at the lowest possible level of the organization – at the point nearest to the problem itself- where the facts of the issue were most readily apparent." (Tidwell, 1985)

Indeed, leaders must inculcate delegation of responsibility at different administrative or leadership levels to establish efficiency in any organization. Trusting, empowering, and delegating duties to other workers within the company, business, church, or institution is a recipe for better organizational success. It is essential to ensure that leaders at the organization's upper echelon focus their time, experience, and expertise on complex and challenging matters that cannot be solved by leaders at the lower level. Delegating responsibilities frees leaders to focus on difficult tasks.

The act of delegating responsibility is a crucial skill necessary for the successful execution of every leadership role. Properly delegating responsibility may be equated to self-duplication. Through the implementation of this skill, a leader is able to bring many of his kind to help do the work.

Later, in Numbers 11:16-18; 24-25 the Lord reiterated and affirmed the importance of this strategy when He took the spirit of Moses and placed it upon seventy elders. Thus, the Lord "duplicated" or delegated the capability of Moses by placing his spirit upon seventy elders, raising seventy Moses-like persons to support him in the implementation of the work. Leadership should not rest on self-execution of every role and responsibility, but rather, identify and surround yourself with competent people who are willing and committed to the organizational vision.

The magnitude of work that was being handled by Moses was so much that God needed to bring in seventy elders to help lighten the burden on Moses. We can easily deduce that Moses was such a hard-working leader and so task-oriented that he had probably lost emotional attachment to the people he was leading. Until this counsel was implemented, Moses did not concern himself with how the people were feeling. If he had empathy with the people, he would have identified the burden his leadership structure had created by causing the people to stand in line all day just to seek redress for simple issues. Apathy for the needs of the people can easily create a huge gap in understanding and providing the right solution.

Some of the reasons why leaders may find it difficult to delegate responsibility include lack of competent resources, insecurity, fear of failure, lack of trust or confidence, lack of planning, fear of losing control, and being too busy to recognize its importance.

This leadership strategy has been adopted and applied successfully across multiple industries, businesses, organizations, churches, nations, and families. Responsibility delegation is essential to establish continuity, improvement, innovations, and ensures long-term sustenance of every organization.

10. CREATE A PATH OF ESCALATION

In wrapping up his recommended leadership strategy to Moses, Jethro highlighted the importance of creating a path of escalation. Escalation defines the process or steps by which higher priority functions or issues are channeled through higher levels of authority. Implementing a path of escalation ensures the execution of timely and effective solutions to problems. In addition, it ensures decisions are made with the right (broader) perspective and authority and provides the framework for enforcing exceptional decisions. Creating a path of escalation or defining an escalation plan ensures that complex issues escape any potential delay of joining a queue and are routed directly to the appropriate level. In Exodus 18:22 NIV, Jethro told Moses, *"But have them bring every difficult case to you."* As a congregational leader, the people were to bring every complex case to Moses to decide. Issues of high importance or magnitude that could not be settled by applying statutes and laws or at the lower levels of the administrative structure were to be escalated to the office of Moses. After teaching the appointed officials the statutes and laws, these leaders were to apply their knowledge to the cases that would come to them. However, there is also the recognition that some cases may have to be settled by discernment, prayer, broader perspective, experience, and/or higher authority. These exceptional cases may go beyond the application of common knowledge or skills.

Moses was to create the path of escalation for these complex cases. By establishing this path, Moses would ensure that every case or challenge would receive the right level of attention. No matter how complicated or straightforward an issue presented itself, there was always an opportunity for redress.

Creating a path of escalation is also a risk management strategy which ensures that potential risks are managed at the right level to avert the potential of becoming issues. Every visionary leader ought to create an escalation plan and implement it for successful handling of issues.

OUTCOME OF JETHRO-MOSES LEADERSHIP MODEL

The above leadership strategies transformed Moses from an inefficient leader to a great and visionary leader who led the people almost to the Promised Land. Jethro drew from his experience to provide practical leadership counsel to Moses with an assurance of the following results. Now let us review the four projected results as indicated by Jethro.

1. LOAD SHARING

The first outcome upon implementing the leadership strategy indicated above is the sharing of roles and responsibilities. By this, the leader alone will not be carrying all the roles and responsibilities, but some of those tasks will be relinquished to others. By involving the people in providing the needed solutions, they will appreciate the impact of their family issues on leadership. In this way, not every issue will burden Moses, since others will share the load.

A visionary leadership structure based on load sharing ensures that opportunity is provided for leadership development, enables the leaders to receive and appreciate the magnitude of issues emanating from their own institutions, and provides an avenue for addressing all issues in a timely manner. It also creates an environment of involvement and amassing support from members. Leadership needs to be intentional in bringing other people on board and providing participation and development opportunities. This involvement should be irrespective of age, gender, race, educational background, tribal or national origin. A diverse representation of leadership composition is essential for identifying issues from different perspectives and providing relevant solutions for the people. A skewed leadership composition may provide a potentially tilted solution that neglects other perspectives, demography, or membership. Visionary leaders must embrace the skill and mindset of sharing roles, responsibilities and authority with others who have the potential in their organizations.

2. PRODUCE LIGHTER LOADS

The second result was that Moses' load would be lighter. Of course, burden sharing makes it lighter. Every visionary leader should find ways to share some of their loads with other leaders. The magnitude of human issues is so complex and sometimes overwhelming that any leader who carries all the burden selfishly does so at their own risk. Many organizational leaders and even ministers of the gospel have resorted to the mindset of Moses. In Exodus 18:15 NIV, Moses gave a very logical and compelling reason to support his practice of unilateral leadership. "Moses answered him, 'Because the people come to me to seek God's will.'" Of course, as a leader, the people will come to you, but it is incumbent on you to embrace the services of other current or potential leaders to provide solutions to the people.

For example, a minister of the gospel may feel compelled to prepare and deliver all sermons and lead prayer sessions, visit and plant churches, execute all the administrative duties, and coordinate with para-church organizations. Some people misconstrue long hours of working as being hardworking. Effective execution of duties does not equate to the duration of engagement. Sharing roles and responsibilities does not make you less of a hard worker but rather positions you for effective delivery. God will intentionally bring onboard potentials, but it is up to the leader to discover the potentials and develop them to perform. A balanced life in leadership is essential to establish quality in delivery. Leaders are discouraged from trading quality for quantity. Programs, activities, and events must be spaced out to ensure the quality of delivery, which is the trademark for a transformative, impactful vision-led ministry.

3. ABILITY TO STAND THE STRAIN

The third result to be achieved is that Moses would have the ability to stand the strain. Once the load is shared, it becomes lighter, exerting less strain on the bearer. Hitherto, Moses alone would bear the heavy burden of the cases from morning until evening and experience complete exhaustion by the end of the day. The people who had to stand all day would go home unhappy and worn out. Implementation of load sharing leadership strategy would prevent overburdening any person, including the leader. The result of shared leadership responsibility is evident here. Leaders who share their roles and responsibilities are less burdened in the execution of their duties. Any visionary leader must purposefully implement this strategy to ensure the maintenance of leadership integrity and instill continuity.

4. PRODUCE SATISFIED FOLLOWERS

Jethro envisioned that successful implementation of his leadership strategy would produce satisfied followers and happy people. Thus, the needs of the people would be met and their issues resolved in a timely fashion. This is because more work will be accomplished within a shorter period with the involvement of other competent people at the right leadership position.

The goal of every visionary leader is to meet the needs of the people. What a blessing to have members of an organization, customers, citizens, and church members experiencing great satisfaction from their needs being met. For example, church members are satisfied when they are fed with the unadulterated Word of God, when there is clear direction from leaders, and when the cloud of prayer is saturated enough to provide protection from the wiles of the enemy and produce enough rain of blessings to flood their spiritual lands. Members are satisfied when they encounter God during church services, prayer meetings, and Bible studies.

It is worth noting that the key to successful leadership revolves around prayerful leaders. Most of the challenges manifested in our churches emanate from the realms of the spirit, and it takes a prayerful leader and intense prayer to quench the fire of social discord from the spiritual realm.

CONCLUSION

Moses obeyed and fully implemented the model recommended by his father-in-law, Jethro. Tidwell clarified that "each suggestion Jethro made is filled with practical wisdom which might come from any objective, intelligent, thoughtful person who was not caught up in busyness that he couldn't take time to think through the problem." Though Jethro must be applauded for thinking through the problem and coming out with such a solid proposition to subdue Moses' inefficiency, it is worth commending Moses for humbling himself to accept his shortfall and fully implementing the counsel of his father-in-law. "Moses listened to his father-in-law and did everything he said." Exodus 18:24 NIV. Apostle Michael Agyemang-Amoako (National Head of COPUSA) said, "It takes a great man or woman to discover the potential in a young person, but it will take the humility of the young person to develop it." Jethro demonstrated his greatness by providing a tangible solution to Moses and transitioning him from just a leader with followers to being a transformative, impactful vision-led leader. Moses received and utilized this opportunity by humbling and availing himself for correction. Nations, organizations, institutions, churches, and families need selfless visionaries and transformative leaders whose legacies will attest to their great leadership styles. Leaders who learn and implement the Moses-Jethro leadership strategies are guaranteed to succeed and make an undeniable impact on society and posterity.

Chapter Summary

- Definition of the Vision of Leadership: Leadership is about influence, the kind that ensures that the leader's vision, and in some cases character, are transplanted into his followers. Jethro gave one of the most powerful and influencing leadership counsels ever recorded in human history to his son-in-law Moses. I have termed this the Jethro-Moses leadership vision/model and have identified ten elements of Jethro's strategic counsel below.

  - Intercede for the people: The first dimension of great Christian leadership is intersession for members. This quality is an expression of leadership empathy, which is indispensable for proper execution of leadership engagement. The ability to represent and meet the needs of the people is the underlying clarion call for both secular and spiritual leaders.

  - Teach them God's decrees/statutes: Humanity is a social entity which influences and is influenced by others. Decrees and statutes seek to establish a framework for human engagement with an intention of promoting social order. The second dimension of great leadership espoused by Jethro was for Moses to impart the right knowledge to facilitate their ability to live with each other.

  - Teach them God's law: Laws are rules and regulations that govern the relationship between an individual or an entity and a higher authority. Usually, laws operate within the scope of authority to ensure smooth engagement between a lower and higher entity. Moses was to teach God's laws to help the people of Israel understand God and establish a relationship with Him.

- Show them the way: Showing them the way implied that Moses was to be an example worthy of emulation by the people. "Since they had the pillar of cloud and fire for their physical direction, this admonition must refer to showing them their life direction as a spiritual counselor." (Tidwell, 1985)

- Show them the work: Jethro's fifth leadership counsel was for Moses to show the people their work. This meant that Moses must communicate clearly and consistently the roles and responsibilities amidst helping them to appreciate their assignment. Leadership must show clarity in the allocation of assignments and help members build performance improvement skills.

- Appoint qualified leaders: The sixth strategy for leadership success was to appoint qualified people to positions of authority. The qualifications included competence, the fear of God, love of the truth, and rejection of covetousness. Any organization, institution, nation, or community that possessess leadership based on these qualities is assured of experiencing a progressively transformative agenda.

- Organize the people and build teams: One of the evidences of effective leadership is the ability to create workable groups or teams within an organization. The seventh strategy for Moses to develop efficiency in his leadership was to organize the people into groups and create manageable, workable, formidable, and productive teams. Efficient leaders ought to adopt and work with teams.

- Empower appointed officials: Although it is important to appoint qualified leaders over groups, it is equally vital to ensure that such leaders are empowered for their respective assignments. Empowerment involves providing the right level of tools, equipment, knowledge, skills, and authority. Striking the right balance between supervision and independence provides prospective leaders opportunity for confidence development. The worldview of empowerment rests on self-discovery, awareness, and developing the power and freedom to explore one's soul, belief, and identity. Christian view of empowerment anchors on reliance on God (the Holy Spirit) to provide capacity for spiritual engagement and exploits.

- Delegate responsibilities: Another strategy for great leadership is the ability to delegate responsibilities to other resources. Delegation is the transfer of responsibility for specific tasks or roles from one person to another. Efficient leadership comes with an appropriate level of delegation.

- Create a path of escalation: Escalation defines the process or steps by which a higher priority functions or issues are channeled through levels of authority for suitable visibility and resolution. Creating a path of escalation ensures the timely and effective execution of solutions to problems, making of decisions and enforcing of such decisions.

- Outcome of Jethro-Moses Leadership Model

    - Great leaders share the responsibility or workload resulting in a lighter load.

    - Great leaders have the ability to stand the strain.

    - Great leaders mostly produce satisfied followers.

CHAPTER FIFTEEN

THE VISION OF ADMINISTRATION - JOSEPH'S VISION

("The great secret about goals and visions is not the future they describe but the change in the present they engender."
- David Allen)

"And there before me was the glory of the God of Israel, as in the vision I had seen in the plain."
Ezekiel 8:4 NIV

VISION STORY - MARTIN LUTHER KING JR.

Martin Luther King Jr. was an American Christian minister, a civil rights activist, and political philosopher. He was born on January 15, 1929, in Atlanta, Georgia and tragically died on April 4, 1968 in Memphis, Tennessee. With over 1000 roads and streets named after him and a federal holiday in his honor, Martin Luther King Jr. inspired millions of people with his unshakable vision of using nonviolent resistance and nonviolent civil disobedience against Jim Crow laws and other forms of legalized discrimination. Inspired by his vision and the civil rights activism of his father Martin Luther King Sr, he participated in and led marches for the right to vote, desegregation, labor rights, and other civil rights. A practiced pastor, he leveraged his vision of a brighter future and his natural speaking ability to liberate millions of people through nonviolent resistance and is known to have delivered one of the finest well-known speeches in the world, "I Have a Dream," effectively communicating his vision to an entire country. As a true visionary leader, Martin Luther King, Jr. made tremendous strides and achieved enviable successes in his fight for civil rights across the United States, through his passion and ability to communicate his vision clearly. The civil rights movement achieved pivotal legislative gains through the Civil Rights Act of 1964, Voting Rights Act of 1965, and the Fair Housing Act of 1968.

INTRODUCTION

One of the most vivid visions conceived and realized in scripture is Joseph's administrative vision, which was birthed out of a dream by Pharaoh. However, this was not the first time Joseph had conceived a vision. At a young age, Joseph had clear multiple visions where he saw himself in a powerful leadership position. The composition and location of his family at that time did not lend itself to the realization of such a vision. Joseph's vision of ascendency and occupancy of a powerful administrative position was a complete deviation from the historical facts of the family. As a family of shepherds, the idea of occupying an authoritative governmental position was far-fetched, yet still, the multiple revelations (Genesis 37: 5, 9) ignited possible fear, hatred, and envy from his siblings and even a rebuke from their father. He glued these visions to his heart and ensured that he became efficient operating in a vision-filled environment. Therefore, Joseph was very comfortable conceiving, interpreting, and sharing visions, the exact situation created by Pharaoh. Joseph was able to interpret the dream with ease and accuracy and went further to craft a unique vision out of Pharaoh's dream. The uniqueness of his vision is that it was crafted to combat potential societal problems of a magnitude that could have easily annihilated an entire nation. The significance and effective implementation of this vision coupled with its remarkable achievement makes it a model for imitation. This administrative vision proposed and implemented by Joseph yielded unimaginable success and presents practical and applicable lessons for our use.

Joseph, a young ex-convict living in a foreign country, was faced with the daunting task of interpreting Pharaoh's dream. By the inspiration of the Spirit of God, Joseph gave an accurate interpretation of Pharaoh's dream. However, my focus here is not on the interpretation of the dream, but the subsequent administrative establishment that ensued, a vision that landed him the job of prime minister. Due to the spiritual underpinning of Joseph's administrative model, I will treat administration from the perspective of the church, but the principles, values, and practices are equally applicable to other institutions and organizations.

Effective administration is essential for the optimal performance of every organization, from the basic institution such as the family unit to the most complex organization like a global conglomerate. They all need a functioning and well-established administration to ensure the optimal utilization of resources. Let us dive deep into church administration and take some lessons from the scriptures.

"Administration of every church must be Christocentric and People Oriented."

Church Administration

Church administration is the art and science of planning, organizing, leading, and harnessing spiritual and physical resources to move the ecclesia toward reaching God's objectives and goals. By this definition, church administration is uniquely different from the administration of other institutions or corporations due to its dual nature, emphasis on both spiritual and physical dimensions of its existence. The Church is not like other institutions (Matthew 16:17-19 NIV) because it is both a spiritual body and a physical organization. "The leadership and guidance required to achieve optimum effectiveness in ...ministry are precisely what comprises the field and function of church administration."[3] Effective administration runs on well-established processes, systems, and procedures.

THE ADMINISTRATIVE HIERARCHY OF THE CHURCH

Every organization has its structure and leadership. At the top of the administration is the CEO/president. Leaders have their vision and objectives that operate within the organization's laid-down principles, constitution, or by-laws. Christ is the owner and head of the Church (Colossians 1:18 NKJV) with a vision that operates within spiritual principles to build the spiritual body, the ecclesia. In the quest of building His Church (Matthew 16:18 NKJV), Christ has chosen and collaborated with men and women (the resources) and have empowered them to equip His Church (Ephesians 4:11-12 NKJV). As we collaborate with our Lord Jesus Christ, He places us in the right department or position based on the need of the Church organization and His prior preparation of the individual. Christ should therefore be the source of every appropriate administrative direction for the Church. Church leaders must recognize that they cannot dwell solely on human principles and values to govern the spiritual body. Every step, process, direction, or strategy applied to church administration must operate within the spiritual framework to yield spiritual results. Church administration must be Christocentric and people oriented.

Christocentric Church Administration

The Church is an earthly representation of the Kingdom of God and should replicate the solid administrative structure in heaven. A Christocentric administration acknowledges Jesus Christ as its foundation (1 Corinthians 3:11 NIV), hinges on Him as its anchor and pillar (Ephesians 2:19-22 NIV), utilizes His principles as its wheels, and relinquishes the driver's seat to the full control of Jesus Christ. The orientation of a Christ-centered administrative model ensures that ministries or programs are fashioned to glorify God (1Corinthians 10:31 NIV) and strengthen one's love for God and each other (Matthew 22: 37-40 NIV). Christocentric church administration ensures and acknowledges that the invisible hand behind the building of the Church is Jesus Christ, though He uses human beings as conduits for that purpose. When Church administration is appropriately deployed and adhered to, people are coherently and cohesively evangelized to Christ, developed to grow and mature in Christ, and equipped to execute ministry for Christ. This is the foundation for the elimination of self-centeredness from any church.

People-Oriented Church Administration

Though the Church is of God, its administration is for the people. In recognizing its humanistic orientation, Tidwell (1985) defined administration as "...enabling them to lead the right people to be at the right place, ..., at the right time, with the right attitudes, knowledge, and skills to perform services that are right to perform."⁷ Church administration must be people oriented because it is executed by people towards people to bring efficiency out of people and enable the organization to achieve an optimal performance of its people. Some disdained administrative establishments have set up processes and systems that are devoid of humanistic composition, which should rather be the focus needed to create the right ecosystems for the Church to achieve its objective. The Church exists to win, prepare, and present people for eternity. Therefore, administrative processes and systems should be knitted with human beings to maintain their importance. Tidwell (1985) identified that "…a major difference between good and poor administration lies in the emphasis the administrator places on people as being more important than things."⁸ Tidwell (1985) The recipe for successfully establishing people-oriented church administration rests on good leadership and human relations.

JOSEPH'S ADMINISTRATIVE VISION

"Now therefore, let Pharaoh select a discerning and wise man, and set him over the land of Egypt. Let Pharaoh do this, and let him appoint officers over the land, to collect one-fifth of the produce of the land of Egypt in the seven plentiful years. And let them gather all the food of those good years that are coming, and store up grain under the authority of Pharaoh, and let them keep food in the cities. Then that food shall be as a reserve for the land for the seven years of famine which shall be in the land of Egypt that the land may not perish during the famine." (Genesis 41: 33-36 NKJV)

When Joseph was presented with the rare opportunity of appearing before Pharaoh to interpret a dream, he did not take that for

---

7 Charles, Tidwell, Church Administration: Effective Leadership for Ministry (29)

8 Ibid, 35

granted. Not only did he interpret the dream, but he also proceeded to recommend a strategic plan of averting the potential disastrous impact of famine on Egypt and other surrounding nations. I have termed Joseph's recommendation and subsequent implementation as the Joseph Administrative Vision/Model and identified five broad categorizations within this model: Resources Identification and Utilization; Planning; Organizing; Directing and Coordinating; and Monitoring and Evaluation.

1. RESOURCE IDENTIFICATION AND UTILIZATION

There are many resources available to every organization, including the church. Identification and allocation of the right resources is a vital prerequisite to the successful implementation of every organization's vision. In our reference scripture, Joseph's first proposition ocenwas focused on resource identification and utilization. If the nation was going to stand against the impending calamity, then it behooved Pharaoh to identify the right resources and place them in the appropriate positions. Such a decision could not be influenced by any defining factor such as race, nationality, age, gender, or background, but by competence. In this particular instance, the only necessary competence was a man in whom was the spirit of God (Genesis 41:38 NIV). If Pharaoh had not looked beyond the human factors mentioned above (Joseph was an ex-convict, 30 years young, and a foreigner) he would have selected an Egyptian who may not have had the grace to execute the assignment rightfully. The result would have been the inevitable famine and the possible destruction of the empire. No family, organization, or nation can develop if they do not recognize and appreciate the valuable resources at their disposal, tap into those resources, and spread their value among its membership. Some of the key resources available to organizations for growth and development are human, natural, physical, intellectual, virtual, financial, and time.

- **The Human Resources** GENESIS 41:33-34 (NIV) The key resource for every organization is its human resources. The souls have been given to the church for its benefit. They are the most valuable resources in the church organization, as they determine the benefits to be derived from all the other resources. Leaders must be intentional in identifying and mentoring resources and provide opportunity for growth.

THREE MAJOR HUMAN RESOURCES

A corporate structure depicts how the company is organized around departments and employees, how they are connected and impacted by each other, and the systems that run their processes. The following are three categories of essential human resources who influence or are influenced by the corporate organization:

- **Shareholders (Owners):** Owners may have been those who started the organization and eventually transitioned it into the hands of the executives or those who invested in the organization through the acquisition of shares. The owners benefit from the value appreciation of the organization or periodic payments in the form of dividends. Jesus Christ is the owner of every church organization (Colossians 1:18; Ephesians 1:22-23 and 4:15) and is the invisible hand behind the building of the Church (Matthew 16:18). Founders of churches must humbly carry the understanding that the actual ownership belongs to Jesus Christ who is building the Church (Christendom) for His glory.

- **Executives:** The growth of an organization usually creates the need for decision-makers, otherwise known as executives or leaders in the corporate world. These categories of employees are brought into the organization to make and facilitate decisions that will move or maintain the company on the path of profitability. As the Church grows, Jesus Christ appoints apostles, prophets, evangelists, pastors, and teachers (Ephesians 4:11-13 NIV), among other leaders, and equips them to equip others for the act of service into growth and maturity. These leaders are empowered to make decisions through the inspiration of the Holy Spirit and lead the ecclesia toward God's objective. "In the Church, the leadership role is performed by persons who are to follow the leadership of Christ... He enables leaders and others to discern the way by means of the Holy Spirit's guidance."[9] The success of the church organization lies on their shoulders, and it is accomplished through the provision of spirit-led decisions. The evolution of complex church organizations, some with appreciable global presence, has triggered the need for effective and efficient executive bodies within such churches. Thus, "ministers and other church leaders find themselves subject to increasing demands for administrative effectiveness."[10] To maintain their relevance and influence on the global spiritual marketplace, such churches must have leaders who have both sound spiritual standing as well as solid administrative acumen. In summary, the grace of such apostles, prophets, evangelists, pastors, teachers, and other leaders must be supported with proper administrative understanding and expertise.

- **General Workers:** The third category of resources is the general workers. Depending on the industry in question, resources within this category may have various levels of task and decision-making combination opportunity. However, they contribute to the greater percentage of work output or service provided.

    - In the context of the Church system, most of the members and workers may fall within this category. This group is the ultimate recipient and focus

---

9 Charles, Tidwell, Church Administration: Effective Leadership for Ministry

10 Charles, Tidwell, Church Administration: Effective Leadership for Ministry

for the administrative establishment and therefore, building administrative structures around them is essential to the success of the church. Every logistical initiation to facilitate smooth operation of the church must keep this group in mind.

- In conclusion, Jesus Christ is the owner of the church organization. He is in the business of building His church for His glory. In the process of executing the business plan, Jesus Christ has employed the clergy and some lay leaders to collaborate for the building of His business. It is therefore vital for the church organization to operate efficiently for optimal performance, grow to profitability (soul winning and spiritual growth) and maintain the status of profitability. This feat can only be achieved if the church organization has a well-established administrative structure and systems for smooth operation. Every church leader/administrator must recognize this vision and work towards its achievement.

Physical Resources: These include the Church buildings, office space, vehicles, equipment, office supplies, and administrative accessories. Resource mobilization and utilization should always be done against the backdrop of true stewardship. We are stewards of God's resources, and we own nothing. Establishment of efficient administration must recognize the importance of this fact, which should ultimately lead to good stewardship. Acquisition of these resources must be accompanied by a good maintenance plan to ensure their optimal usage and longevity.

Financial Resources: Financial resources are funds and other financial assets that finance an organization's activities and investments. Tithes and offerings are some of the main sources of financial resources for the church. Proper financial stewardship should be executed within the scope of budgeting, revenue generation, expenses, and cost management. Funds solicited must be used for their intended purpose to avoid any possibility of misappropriation (Acts 5:1-10 NKJV). The purpose of church funding is for the expansion of the Kingdom of God and must be used as such. Therefore, chief stewards (ministers) must desist from enriching themselves with church funds.

Time Resources: Time is an irretrievable and limited resource. Every effort must be channeled towards the proper management of time in every circumstance. Meeting times, duration of services, and other engagements are to be managed to cut down every wastage.

- **Intellectual Resources:** Intellectual resources are assets that are based on knowledge, information, or other intangible assets. This may include knowledge, skills, expertise, organizational processes and procedures, trademarks, patents, copyrights, trade secrets, and business relationships. Most church organizations are heavily endowed with intellectual resources. Such churches should make every effort to harness and preserve their intellectual resources for growth and as an asset for the organization.

- **Technological and Virtual Resources:** Technological and virtual resources have become essential tools for the growth of any organization, including churches. The use of social media, the internet, and other virtual space is critical for timely dissemination of information to both current and prospective members. Social media platforms provide opportunities for continued engagement with the outside world even from the comfort of our homes and offices. This resource should be explored for the propagation of the gospel.

2. PLANNING: GENESIS 41:37 NIV "THE PLAN SEEMED GOOD TO PHARAOH AND TO ALL HIS OFFICIALS."

Planning is the process of identifying and documenting all the activities needed to achieve a goal or vision. Interestingly, the Bible indicates that the plan seemed good to Pharaoh and his officials, meaning, Joseph did not only present an interpretation but also a valuable plan to curtail the impending disaster. A careful study of the account of creation reveals that creation followed a well thought out plan (Genesis 1). The sequence of creation was implemented in an orderly manner, which I believe was based on a plan. I believe one of the reasons why Joseph's administration experienced great success was his ability to plan before execution. Ministries or churches must operate with a good, well thought out plan to ensure success. A good plan should be flexible to adapt to change during its course of implementation. It is essential that a plan, including that of the church, is well communicated to members of the organization for an adequate level of understanding. The following are some advantages for planning and executing a plan for ministries.

i. Planned ministries lead to progress and alleviate repetition.

ii. Planning builds continuity in the church's program.

iii. Through planning, synergies in ministries are identified and leveraged.

iv. Through planning, the support of the membership is amassed for implementation.

v. Through planning, potential risks are identified for mitigation.

3. ORGANIZING: (GENESIS 41:35-36; EXODUS 18:21-26; NEHEMIAH 3)

Organizing is the process of coordination and allocation of tasks and activities to resources within an organization. During the process of organizing, managers coordinate tasks, activities, employees, resources, policies, and procedures towards the realization of a common vision or objective. This process may involve identification and allocation of tasks to individuals and departments, delegation of authority, allocation of resources across the organization, developing an organizational structure to facilitate smooth supervision, and exercise of authority. The goal of organizing is to ensure the smooth running of an organization for the achievement of a common goal, objective, or vision.

Companies are mostly organized in three dimensions: divisional, functional, and matrix.

Divisional organization:ach division functions on its own. Each division may be organized based on either product line or geographical location, with their own functional departments. Product departmentalization is when various activities related to the product or service are under the authority of one manager, while geographic departmentalization involves grouping activities based on location under the management of one person.

Functional Organization: Under functional structure, an organization is divided into subgroups based on their functions or areas of specialty, such as finance, marketing, and IT. Under this structure, companies' top management is made up of various functional heads such as chief finance officer and chief operating officer. Functional organizations offer greater operational efficiency, since individuals with common skill sets are grouped together to operate independently under management with the same skill set. Here, management acts as the point of cross-communication between functional areas

Matrix Organization: Under this structure, individuals are grouped by two different operational areas at the same time. Here, companies are organized by various organizations' perspectives, which may include function and product, function and region, or region and product.

Under Joseph's organizational structure, officers were appointed and placed over various geographical areas to ensure that 20% of grain was collected and stored in the cities. All these officers were to operate under the supervision of the discerning and wise man (Joseph) but under the authority of Pharaoh. Joseph was in charge of all the land of Egypt (Genesis 41:43 NIV) and he traveled throughout Egypt, but the officers were in charge of smaller geographical areas with the cities as their storage centers.

4. DIRECTING AND COORDINATION

This involves supervision, management, and control of resources.

Directing: It is a strategy used by leadership to captivate followers, guide, inspire, lead, and motivate them to achieve the organizational goals. Directing is one of the most important functions of management that helps employees to know the path to achieving the organizational goals and vision effectively and efficiently. Without directing, some employees may be clueless about the right path towards the organization's objective.

Coordinating: According to Mooney and Reelay, "Coordination is the orderly arrangement of group efforts to provide unity of action in the pursuit of common goals." It involves aligning and harmonizing various activities, resources, and individuals to ensure smooth running of operations and achievement of desired outcomes. It requires excellent organizational, leadership and communication skills, and the ability to align multiple moving parts towards a common goal.

Joseph exhibited his directing and coordination skills by traveling throughout the land of Egypt and working with his subordinates to gather and store immeasurable food in the cities during the seven years of abundance (Genesis 41:46-49 NIV). Food was gathered from surrounding towns and villages and kept in granaries in various cities. This was necessary to ensure that storage and distribution centers were as close to the people as possible, cutting down the duration and distance of travel during both the gathering and distribution. By traveling throughout Egypt, Joseph also ensured that the right tasks were completed through managerial supervision, directing the people to work appropriately, and coordinating the activities of multiple locations to ensure the goal of having enough grains stored at strategic locations was achieved.

5. MONITORING AND EVALUATION

The final step in the administrative process is monitoring and evaluation. It is the process of assessing the vision's outcomes to determine the extent or magnitude of achievement and impact. **Monitoring:** An ongoing process that tracks progress against its objectives. The implementation of every vision should be monitored to determine the level of progress against intended outcomes. Monitoring uses methods such as data collection, analysis, and reporting to provide relevant information for decision-making and improvement. Monitoring is a continuous process throughout the vision implementation phases and it is also essential to alleviate the possibility of drifting off course.

Evaluation: This is the process of measuring progress against established standards. Evaluation uses methods such as surveys, interviews, reports, and case studies to assess the quality, relevance, and sustainability of the chosen path towards the vision's realization. The evaluation process is an analysis or interpretation of collected data which delves deeper into the relationships between the results, the effects produced, and the overall impact of the project towards the vision.

Biblical Application

Joseph's administrative model included continuous monitoring and evaluation. In addition to directing and coordinating the activities for the building of silos, collection, and storage of the grains, Joseph's presence ensured that he was able to monitor the progress of work and evaluate the effectiveness and efficiency of the adopted strategy. His presence at the grassroots granted him real time and first-hand information in evaluating the progress of the work.

Monitoring and evaluating the work of ministry is an important step in church administration. The aforementioned administrative structure established by Joseph is an adaptable model for building church administrations.

CONCLUSION

One of the most transformative visions conceived and implemented in the Bible is that which was born out of Pharaoh's dream. Pharaoh needed someone to interpret his dream but could not find anyone in his kingdom other than a foreigner by the name of Joseph, who was languishing in the Egyptian jail for a crime he did not commit. Upon his arrival, Joseph interpreted the dream and proceeded to present a plan that could minimize the potential impact of an impending famine. The implementation of Joseph's administrative vision ensured that the right resources were identified to establish an efficient administrative structure. It also provided the opportunity for food to be collected and stored during the seven years of abundance as well as the distribution of stored food during the subsequent seven years of famine. Joseph's administrative model is implementable in different organizations and institutions, including the church. The process of identifying and using the right resources, planning, organizing, directing, and coordinating, monitoring and evaluation is a model administrative process, applicable and useful in our time. I have included this as one of the uniquely impactful and transformative visions in scripture for the implementation of church leaders.

Chapter Summary

Introduction to Administration: The three main perspectives of administration include leadership, management, and processes or systems.

Church administration is the art and science of planning, organizing, leading, and harnessing both spiritual and physical resources to move the ecclesia toward reaching God's objective and goals. The Church, being both a spiritual organization and physical institution, occupies a spiritual position, which underscores its physical standing.

- The Administrative Hierarchy of the church: Jesus Christ is the owner and head of every church with a vision that operates within spiritual principles to build a spiritual body. Church administration must be both Christocentric and people-oriented.

- Christocentric Administration: A Christocentric church administration acknowledges Jesus Christ as its foundation and pillar, utilizes His values and principles, and relinquishes the driver's seat for His full control.

- People-Oriented Administration: Though the church is of God, its administration is for the people. Church administration must be people-oriented because it is established and executed by people towards people to bring efficiency out of the people for an optimal performance of the people.

Joseph's Administrative Vision: Identified below are the five main administrative strategies established by Joseph.

- Identification and Utilization of Resources: Some of the resources available for churches include human, physical, financial, time, intellectual, and technological/virtual. All these resources should be leveraged for the establishment and growth of the church.

- Planning: Identifies and documents activities needed to achieve goals or visions. Planning church activities is a recipe for success and ensures progress, alleviation of repetition, continuity, leveraging of synergies, amassing the support of membership, identification and mitigation of risks.

- Organizing: The process of coordination and allocation of tasks and activities to resources within an organization.

- Directing and Coordinating: Involves supervision, management and control of resources.

- Monitoring and Evaluation: This final step in administration is the process of assessing the vision's outcome to determine the extent or magnitude of achievement and impact.

CHAPTER SIXTEEN

VISION OF DOMINANCE (JESUS' VISION)

("A great leader's courage to fulfill his vision comes from passion, not position." - John Maxwell)

"Therefore go and make disciples of all nations, baptizing them in the name of the Father and of the Son and of the Holy Spirit."

Matthew 28:19 NIV

VISION STORY-HENRY FORD

One of the most accomplished business leaders in history is Henry Ford, the man credited with transforming automobile production operations and revolutionizing both transportation and American industry. With his introduction of the automobile assembly line, he made mass production of automobiles possible. Henry Ford was born on July 30, 1863 in a farmhouse in Michigan's Springwells Township, leaving home at age 16 to find work in Detroit. During the late 1880s, Ford began repairing and later constructing engines; however, he was always driven by a strong vision. In 1903, the vision compelled him to start the Ford Motor Company with virtually none of his own money but rather, harnessed his vision to negotiate deals and reinvest his profits.

With the creation of the assembly line, his successful business practices, and a vision that inspired thousands, Ford cemented himself as a legend in the business world.

His business principle, "Fordism," is an industrial engineering and manufacturing system that serves as the basis of modern social and labor-economic systems that support industrialized, standardized mass production and mass consumption. His work not only transformed the automobile industry, but also revolutionized the entire business landscape in America. His is a legacy that has thrived and persisted for over a century.

INTRODUCTION

"The vision of Jesus Christ is the greatest vision ever conceived and executed in the history of humanity."

This book on vision would be incomplete without due consideration to the vision of Jesus Christ. By all accounts, Jesus' vision is the greatest vision ever conceived and executed in the history of humanity. I have termed this as the vision of dominance. This vision was so great and impactful that the world timeline was established with Jesus' birth as the reference point. There is no kingdom, nation, institution, or any form of human grouping that has sustainably maintained its relevance and dominance on the global marketplace of impartation over the course of history as has Christendom. The magnitude of the qualitative impact of Christ's vision on humanity will be reserved for another day's discussion; however, a glimpse of the quantitative impact is evidenced in the current religious world. The website worldpopulationreview.com estimates that a little less than a third (2.4 billion people out of about 8 billion) of the world's population are Christians. However, if we compare this number against the vision of Christ, of making disciples of ALL NATIONS (Matthew 28:19), then we come to the realization that we still have a long way to go. The vision is that all nations (the entire 8 billion-plus world population) would become disciples of our Lord Jesus Christ. So the vision realization indicator is when all nations have become disciples of Jesus Christ. At that point, Christians can confidently say the vision has been realized. But until then, Christians should still be on the move and must employ the very strategy espoused in the ministry of Jesus. The strategic model of Jesus' vision can be categorized below:

SELF-EQUIPING AND EMPOWERMENT

EQUIPPING AND EMPOWERING OTHERS (DISCIPLESHIP)

TEAM FORMATION

UNLEASHING TO THE WORLD

SELF-EQUIPING AND EMPOWERMENT

Jesus spent the first thirty years of His earthly life equipping Himself with the prerequisite knowledge and skills for ministry and empowering Himself for successful spiritual engagement. No wonder, that by the time He stepped out into the limelight, He was fully equipped and empowered for success. Let us review His self-equipping and empowerment.

KNOWLEDGE AND SKILL ACQUISITION

The first step of Jesus positioning Himself towards the achievement of His vision was knowledge and skill acquisition. At the early age of twelve, Jesus was found in the temple among teachers of the law, listening, asking questions, and offering valuable contributions (Luke 2:41-47 NKJV). The activity of knowledge gathering falls under the preparatory phase while skills development occurs within the gestational phase of vision development (Luke Chapter 6). It is obvious from the scripture above that His pursuit of knowledge preceded the occurrence of His engagement with the teachers of the law. This is because everyone who heard Him at that age was amazed by His level of understanding as evidenced in His answers. The boy Jesus had acquired knowledge to equip Himself for the impending task of ministry. It is said that proper preparation prevents poor performance. Success is when opportunity meets preparation. Proper preparation is the initial step towards the achievement of success in any venture. Jesus asking questions in the Temple and sitting among the teachers was the strategy of equipping Himself with the right level of knowledge before stepping out into the public. The Apostle Paul reiterated this call towards his mentee, Timothy. Simple inference from this scripture is that preparation in the form of knowledge acquisition is even essential for receiving approval from God. The workman who aspires for God's approval must study. The employee who needs attestation from his superior or the adventurous person who needs validation from his environment must study.

Among other things, success in ministry is knowledge-based. The vision for Christianity to dominate the world ought to be pursued with proper understanding through careful teachings of new and old converts alike.

EQUIP IN PRIVATE FOR PUBLIC DISPLAY

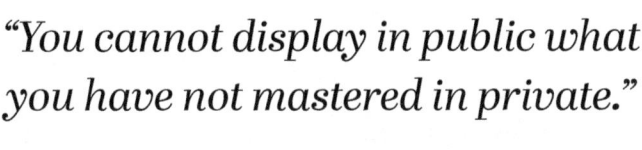

"You cannot display in public what you have not mastered in private."

One of the common setbacks in Christendom is the prevalence of ill-prepared or unprepared ministers occupying leadership positions in churches. This has resulted in misinterpretation of scripture and development of divergent and sometimes false doctrines. The issue has been compounded by the emergence of and access to social media, which has created the opportunity for anyone with a smart phone and the internet to post any of such teachings unto the world. Unfortunately, some of those people have almost no understanding of scripture but prey upon the emotions and ignorance of people to gather followers. We clearly read that at the age of 12 (probably younger) Jesus was studying the art, skill, and strategies for ministry. This equipped Him to fully understand and appreciate the full dimension, potential challenges, and nuances of ministry before announcing His ministry publicly. So the question is, will you receive medical attention from an untrained medical officer or receive knowledge from an ill-prepared teacher? Why do people sit under the feet of people who profess to be ministers but do not have the requisite knowledge? Receiving knowledge from the right source is essential to raising and molding Christ-like characters.

Another great lesson here is that Jesus did not announce His vision until age thirty, which means that He spent a minimum of eighteen years before launching His ministry. This is food for thought for young prospective ministers. Your time of preparation is not wasted, but rather an investment with direct bearing on your prospect of success, so prepare yourself before announcing yourself.

SPIRITUAL EMPOWERMENT

Another area Jesus prepared Himself for success was empowering himself spiritually. Jesus, full of the Holy Spirit, moved away from River Jordan and was led by the Spirit into the wilderness where He defeated the devil during the period of temptation (Luke 4:1-13 NKJV). Jesus' deep knowledge of the Word of God was very instrumental in conquering the devices and misapplication of the Word of God by Satan. Jesus empowered Himself spiritually before the commencement of His ministry by embarking on forty days of fasting and prayer. He also continuously empowered Himself through frequent prayer, fasting and periodic solitude for effective and engaging spiritual exercise.

In fact, Jesus recommended this same strategy of empowerment to His disciples. He stressed the importance of spending time with the Holy Spirit after understanding Him through His teachings. This was an important contributing factor to the success of their future ministries. They had to privately commune with the Holy Spirit before publicly announcing their ministry to the world. They were asked to wait in Jerusalem until they had received the gift of the Father, the Holy Spirit, our source of empowerment, before departing into the world (Acts 1:4-5 NIV). This command still stands and applies to anyone who desires success in the execution of his or her ministerial journey.

There are countless oppositions and challenges on the path to ministerial success. Overcoming them requires adequate and continuous preparation, as well as reliance on God's grace. This is because any spiritually empowered leader is a lethal weapon in the hands of God and a threat to the camp of the enemy. Satan does not take such people lightly at all. No wonder Satan deployed all possible forms of temptation and sources of spiritual weakness, such as the lust of the eye, the lust of the flesh, and the pride of life (1 John 2:16 NIV), against Jesus (Matthew 4:1-11 NIV) to lure Him into sin. Thanks be to God, Jesus had equipped Himself to successfully stand against such wiles of Satan through appropriate application of the knowledge of scripture.

I want to encourage current and prospective Church leaders to patiently equip themselves with knowledge of the scriptures and empower themselves spiritually to effectively execute their task as authentic spiritual leaders. Self-equipping and empowerment were undertaken by Jesus and the apostles, and all dynamic, impactful, and relevant spiritual leaders throughout history have followed suit.

TEAM FORMATION

After Jesus completed His personal ministerial formation, He then embarked on team formation. He called His twelve apostles (Luke: 12-16 NIV), who were His vision partners, and subsequently gathered His disciples. Jesus sought divine enablement by spending time in prayer before the team formation. He brought people from outside the status quo (not rabbis) to achieve a vision, which deviated from the norm of the day. Hull emphasized, "When Jesus launched His ministry, He bypassed the religious professionals of His day, choosing instead to recruit twelve ordinary laymen from different walks of life. To these men, who lacked the rigidity of spirituality, He presented the opportunity of a different kind of ministry. Through those who have not received the training of the rabbis or the prestige of the priesthood, He said, 'You shall be the salt of the earth, the light of the world.'" (Matthew 5:13-16 NIV)

The composition of the team included people from diverse backgrounds such as commoners, fishermen (Matthew 4:18-22 NIV), a tax collector (Matthew 4:18-22 NIV, Luke 5:27- 28 NIV), politicians, and the educated and not so educated. The diverse background was strategic and necessary to cater to the needs of the entire society, ensuring that no class of people were left unattended. With the expansion of many Pentecostal and Charismatic churches and their attainment of global status, it is imperative that "strategic diversification" in leadership formation is pursued. My use of the phrase "strategic diversification" should not be misconstrued to mean the kind of inclusivity being promoted by some countries within the Western Hemisphere. Here, my focus is rather on the formation of a leadership team based on competence and grace and in consideration of the geographical footprint of the church organization. In other words, the leadership composition for these global churches should be reflective of its global membership, so that decision making will embrace wisdom from multiple perspectives and backgrounds. Jesus' leadership team was well diversified, which ensured that His ministry did not appeal only to a certain class of society at the expense of others.

The scope of Jesus' vision is global dominance and could not have been achieved unilaterally. This called for the formation of a competently committed team, sharing of the vision, and amassing their support for execution. For global Church leadership, diversity is particularly important to enable its members to work with people of diverse backgrounds, without compromising on their morality, spirituality, values, and principles of the Kingdom of God.

EQUIPPING AND EMPOWERING OTHERS (DISCIPLING)

One of the uniquenesses of Jesus' ministry was His quest to equip and empower His followers. The hallmark of His earthly ministry hinges on an instructive model of equipping, empowering, and releasing others. He told His disciples right from the beginning that He would make them "fishers of men." (Matthew 4:19 NIV) For that to happen, Jesus had to transform their vision as fishermen into fishers of men by imparting the true knowledge and unveiling the true perspective of the Kingdom of God. Each step of the way, among other lessons, Jesus taught them how to pray (Luke 11:1-4 NIV), fast properly (Matthew 6:16-18 NIV), model discipleship (John 13:1–5 NIV), connect people to God (Matthew 28:19-20 NIV), have faith in God (Mark 11:22-25 NIV), and to make peace with others (Matthew 5:9 NIV). Jesus continued to expand their vision through the assurance that by believing in Him, the disciples were positioned to do greater things than what He had accomplished (John 14:12 NIV). In other words, embracing, employing, and applying His strategies may result in a greater scope of accomplishment.

All the essential elements of equipping, namely the impartation of knowledge, delegation of authority (Luke 10:19 NIV), spiritual empowerment (John 14, 15,16 NIV), and assurance of continuous support (Matthew 28:20 NIV) have all been met and demonstrated through the ministry of Jesus Christ. He taught in private and in public; no wonder after spending just about three and half years with Christ, the disciples were abreast with the teachings of the Kingdom of God. The outpouring of the Holy Spirit on the day of Pentecost marked the final stage of their empowerment. This final stage was essential to ensure that His followers were adequately prepared, equipped, and empowered before launching out.

PAUL'S EQUIPPING KNOWLEDGE

The Apostle Paul also took up the same model as Christ of equipping others. "From the time of his earliest team relationship as an associate to Barnabas (Acts 11:19-20) at Antioch, Paul practiced and taught an equipping ministry. Strong and superbly qualified as he was for singular leadership, Paul saw the essential wisdom of a shared ministry." (Tidwell, 85) Paul equipped Timothy and Silas (Acts 17:14-15) by giving them the opportunity to minister and to handle the growing church in Berea. Clearly, Paul had caught the vision of equipping initiated by Jesus Christ.

To ensure that the vision was vividly transferred to other churches and understood throughout generations, Paul presented the equipping ministry vision to the church in Ephesus. "So Christ himself gave the apostles, the prophets, the evangelists, the pastors and teachers, to equip his people for works of service, so that the body of Christ may be built up." (Ephesians 4:11-12 NIV) Paul expressed unequivocally that the purpose for which Christ established those ministerial callings is to continue the implementation of His vision of equipping others. The same should be executed "until we all attain to unity in faith and to perfect knowledge of the Son of God and become mature, attaining to the whole measure of the fullness of Christ." (Ephesians 4:13 NIV)

This vision of equipping and empowering is the model vision of continuity and worthy of emulation. Leadership of any organization that desires sustainability and continuity can adopt and implement this vision for guaranteed longevity of their organization. Christianity has stood the test of time and continues to make inroads into the world partly because of this model. Transcending from one generation to another, ordinary people are called, imparted with the knowledge of the Kingdom of God, empowered through spiritual engagement and repositioning, and released into the world to repeat the cycle. Church leaders should be intentional in identifying young people, equipping and empowering them, and subsequently assigning the right responsibility for their pursuit. This is how the Kingdom of God will continue to expand and the vision of making disciples of all nations will come to fruition.

WELL-DEFINED ASSIGNMENT

Jesus clearly defined and assigned responsibilities to His followers. This helped the disciples to perform tasks exactly as they were supposed to, and to demonstrate the love of God to the world. The disciples were given a direct assignment from Jesus to go and "make disciples of all nations." How were they supposed to accomplish this assignment? By "teaching them to obey everything" Jesus had taught them, baptizing them "in the name of the Father and of the Son and of the Holy Spirit." (Matthew 28:19-20 NIV) Any assignments given by church leaders must be devoid of ambiguities so that those who are working with them will have clear directions to perform their duties. Sometimes great endeavors are accomplished through simple means. Simplicity is a weapon for making remarkable strides. Assignment definition and allocation should be channeled through the means of simplicity to avoid potential ambiguity.

DELEGATION OF AUTHORITY

At the end of Jesus' ministerial journey on earth, He ensured that the vision of dominance was well articulated and firmly established in the hearts of His followers. Indeed, He had spent a considerable amount of time equipping and empowering His disciples, and now the mantle was going to fall on them. The thing they needed the most was authority for the furtherance of the Kingdom. So we read, "Then Jesus came to them and said, 'All authority in heaven and on earth has been given to me.'" (Matthew 28:18 NIV) He then delegated that authority to both present and prospective believers. He was intentional and strategic in the delegation and reminded believers that His mission on earth was also through delegated authority. Jesus was sending His disciples just as His Father had sent Him (John 20:21 NIV). He commissioned the apostles to proclaim the gospel, heal the sick, cleanse the lepers, raise the dead, and cast out demons (Matthew 10:5–8 NKJV). All these signs were to serve as "advertisements" that would draw people's attention and lead them to become members of the Kingdom.

The vision is that ALL NATIONS MUST BE DISCIPLED TO CHRIST. The current 30%, or 50%, 80% or even 90% is still not the vision. The vision is 100% global citizenship discipled to Christ. This vision is clear, time-bound (though believers are not told of the exact time per Mark 13:32), solution-bound, and measurable. Jesus Christ gave us the blueprint for achieving this vision: equip and empower yourself, step out to equip and empower others, grant them the opportunity to further equip and empower themselves, and let the cycle continue. This way, at any point in time, there are believers who have been equipped and empowered, others who are being equipped and empowered, and prospective candidates to follow this cycle. This cycle is the bedrock of Jesus' vision, which is very simple yet powerful and seeks to ensure sustainability and continuity until Christendom dominates and becomes the only religion across the nations.

This clarion call is still ringing through the church bells, "Hark! the voice of Jesus calling,

'Who will go and work today?' Fields are white, and harvests waiting; Who will bear the sheaves away? Loud and long the Master calleth, Rich reward he offers free; Who will answer, gladly saying, 'Here am I; send me, send me.'"

Chapter Summary

- Jesus Christ's vision (the Vision of Dominance) by all accounts is the greatest vision ever conceived and executed in the history of humanity. This is because there is no kingdom, nation, institution, or any human grouping that has sustainably maintained its relevance and dominance on the global marketplace of impartation and transformation as has Christendom. The vision is that all nations shall be discipled to Jesus.

- To accomplish the vision above, Jesus Christ strategically equipped Himself with knowledge and skills of ministry during His formative years. He also empowered Himself by fasting, praying, and engaging in other spiritual exercises.

- Jesus Christ prepared His disciples to pursue this vision by equipping and empowering them through discipleship, formed their teams, defined their assignments, delegated authority, and discharged them into the world.

- Believers are called to employ this strategy to disciple the whole world unto Christ.

CHAPTER SEVENTEEN

VISION CONCLUSION

("If you create a vision for your life, doors will open."
Anonymous)

"I, Daniel, was worn out. I lay exhausted for several days. Then I got up and went about the king's business. I was appalled by the vision; it was beyond understanding."

Daniel 8:27 NIV

VISION STORY- NELSON MANDELA

Nelson Mandela was South Africa's first democratically elected president (1994-1999). He was a revolutionary and political leader, who was appreciated worldwide for his commitment to peace negotiation and reconciliation. He was a philanthropist with a genuine, unceasing love for children, a Nobel Peace Prize winner, and an anti-apartheid leader who spent 27 years in prison for holding onto a noble vision. His vision to end apartheid and its associated crimes committed by the white minority in South Africa was inspired by the story of his ancestors' valor during the wars of resistance. Despite multiple twists and turns, his vision came to fruition about half a century later when at the age of 77 he became president, experiencing the manifestation of the vision he conceived as a teenager.

CONCLUSION

Many transformative forces seek to define and influence an individual's understanding and perspective of life. One such force is the valor of vision. Vision has an intrinsically strong capability to compel individuals or society to identify, appreciate, explore, and utilize resources at their disposal, resulting in a higher standard of living. The absence of vision equally has a strong propensity of denial and can deprive people from recognizing and appreciating available resources within their domain. It is against this backdrop that understanding the topic of vision and its inherent proficiency is a game changer, an eye opener, and a force for deriving optimal benefits from resources towards the attainment of greatness.

It is said that understanding makes everything easier. Therefore, treating the characteristics that define a good vision ensures that readers of this book have been equipped to translate their preliminary ideas into clear, achievable, measurable, time-bound and solution-bound visions for proper understanding by the heralds. Such invaluable information contributes towards establishing the scope of a vision.

I categorized vision into two main forms, namely, personal and corporate, based on the primary beneficiary agent. Therefore, the primary beneficiary of personal vision is an individual, whereas that of a corporate vision is an organization, nation, or society. Through this book, I also identified vision as sight, soulish, and spiritual. Sight is perceived through the agency of the eye and its related organs. Soulish visions are conceived through either emotion, will, or intellect. This type of vision (soulish) is conceived through triggers that affect the aforementioned composition of the soul. The third type of vision (spiritual) is only possible for spiritual individuals and usually originates from a deity or divine powers. The knowledge unearthed through the categorization of vision provides the encouragement and assurance that any person is capable of conceiving and manifesting a vision.

The holy grail of vision attainment is not only in its conception, but also the ability to recognize its value and transmit it through proper phases of growth such as conception, preparatory, gestation, and realization. Equally important is the knowledge and skill of managing dormancy. The teachings on the nature and characteristics of vision established a framework of deeper understanding and appropriate engagement to facilitate amiable interaction between the vision, individuals, and society. This is critical in confirming that conceived visions are not aborted or birthed prematurely, the cause of many failed visions. Pertinent to human failure is also lack of vision, which ensures the absence of direction, destination, discipline, leadership, inspiration, and purpose.

I dedicated the second part of this book to treating specific groundbreaking Biblical visions as a model for our emulation. This includes the visions of greatness, success, leadership, administration, and dominance. Inherent in these Biblical visions are strategic applicable models capable of producing the kind of results experienced by its bearers. Therefore, the ability to adopt and adapt to these models will set you on the path of encountering similar outcomes. However, one of the profoundly distinguishing features in the realization of these Biblical visions is their spirituality dependence. All the visions eventually culminated into Jesus' vision of dominance, which is the greatest vision by all standards and dimensions. The vision of dominance provides a perfect example for ensuring sustenance and continuity.

The inclusion of real-life stories throughout the book was to provide diverse perspectives of visions. These real-life stories attest to the achievability of visions, irrespective of people's background, gender, circumstances, challenges, or capabilities.

As you finalize your interaction with this book, my hope is that you have been given enough ammunition for proper conception, nurturing, and birthing of your vision. Now that you have been equipped, step up and step out, with your vision as your North Star. Pursue it relentlessly and you will soon arrive at the destination of manifestation. It is my prayer that the remarkable level of success experienced by the visionaries in this book, along with the knowledge unveiled, will serve as an unceasing source of inspiration to persistently propel you towards your vision.

SELECTED BIBLIOGRAPHY

Allen, David, Ready for Anything: 52 Productivity Principles for Work and Life (Simon & Schuster, 2019)

Anderson, Allan Heaton, To the Ends Of The Earth: Pentecostalism and The Transformation of World Christianity (Oxford University Press, 2013)

Carnegie, Dale, How to Win Friends & Influence People (Pocket Books, 1998)

Clear, James, Atomic Habits: An Easy & Proven Way to Build Good Habits & Break Bad Ones (Neha Publishers & Distribution, 2022)

Cole, A Graham, He who Gives Life: The Doctrine of the Holy Spirit. (Crossway Wheaton, IL, 2007)

Corvin, Douglas, Visions and Dreams: This is The Time (1993)

Fortune, Don & Katie, Discover Your God-Given Gifts. Revised and Expanded Edition (Green Press Initiative, 2009)

Franklin, Jentezen, Believe That You Can: It's Time to Make It Happen (Charisma House, 2002)

Greene, Robert, The Laws of Human Nature (Viking, 2018)

Groeschel, Craig, Think Ahead: 7 Decisions You Can Make Today for the God-Honoring Life You Want Tomorrow (Zondervan, 2024)

Herold, Cameron, Vivid Vision: A Remarkable Tool For Aligning Your Business Around a Shared Vision of the Future (Lioncrest Publishing, 2017)

Hill, Napoleon, Think and Grow Rich

Hyatt, Michael, The Vision Driven Leader: 10 Questions to Focus Your Efforts, Energize Your Team, and Scale Your Business (Baker Books, 2020)

Inamori, Kazuo, A Passion for Success: Practical, Inspirational, and Spiritual Insight from Japan's Leading Entrepreneur (McGraw-Hill, Inc., 1995)

Jakes, T.D, Life Overflowing, 6 Pillars for Abundant Living (Bethany House, 2010)

Kadavy, David, Mind Management, Not Time Management: Productivity When Creativity Matters (Kadavy, Inc. 2020)

Konovalov, Oleg, Vivid Vision: A Remarkable Tool For Aligning Your Business Around a Shared Vision of the Future (John Wiley & Sons Inc, 2021)

Lotich, Patricia, Smart Church Management: A Quality Approach to Church Administration, Third Edition (2020)

Lynch, Richard, Focus on Reading (2006)

Migliore, L. Daniel, Faith Seeking Understanding: An Introduction to Christian Theology, Third Edition (William B. Eerdmans Publishing Company Grand Rapids, Michigan/Cambridge, U.K, 2014

Monroe, Myles, Uncover your potential: You are More than you realize (Destiny Image Publishers Inc. 2012)

Onyinah, Opoku, Spiritual Warfare, Third Edition (Pentecost Press, 2016)

SELECTED BIBLIOGRAPHY

Poore, Carol, Leadership in the Metaverse: Creating the Future of WebWe Through Strategy and Community Building (Fast Company Press, 2022)

Powers P. Bruce, Church Administration Handbook, Third Edition (B&H Academic, 2008)

Shallenberger, Steven & Rob, Start with the Vision: Six Steps to Effectively Plan, Create Solutions, and Take Action (2020)

Tidwell, Charles, Church Administration Effective Leadership for Ministry (B&H Academic, 1985)

Turner, Max, Holy Spirit and Spiritual Gifts: In the New Testament Church and Today, Revised Edition (Baker Academic, 2012)

Welch, H. Robert, Church Administration: Creating Efficiency for Effective Ministry, Second Edition (B&H Academic, 2011)

Whetstone V. Gary, It Only Takes One (Whitaker House, 2003)

Williams, J. Rodman, Renewal Theology, Vol. 2. (Grand Rapids: Zondervan Publishing House, 1990)

Wimberly, Jr. W. John, The Business of the Church: The Uncomfortable Truth that faithful Ministry Requires Effective Management (The Alban Institute, 2010)

ABOUT THE AUTHOR

GODFRED DODZIE AMUZU

Godfred Dodzie Amuzu is an ordained Prophet of The Church of Pentecost. He is the National Administrative Manager of the Church of Pentecost USA and the District Minister for Pentecost International Worship Center (PIWC) in Orange, New Jersey. He was called into full-time ministry in 2015, to the pastorate in 2019, and into the office of a Prophet in 2023. He served as the District Pastor for Phoenix Arizona District from 2015 to 2018. He is currently a member of the National Finance Board, National Risk Management Committee, and the secretary of the National Pension Board.

Prophet Godfred Dodzie Amuzu holds a Bachelor of Science degree from Kwame Nkrumah University of Science and Technology, a diploma of Theological and Pastoral Studies from the Pentecost Biblical Seminary, and a Master of Business Administration (MBA) in Finance & Investment from Oklahoma City University. He holds an advanced certificate in Project Management from Boston University and a Project Management Professional (PMP) with the Global Project Management Institute.

Prior to his calling into full-time ministry, Prophet Godfred Dodzie Amuzu spent over a decade in corporate finance and investments, having held various leadership positions at fortune 500 companies such as JP Morgan Chase, TD Bank, Fannie Mae and Barclays Bank. He is the author of the book, *The Valor of Vision*. Prophet Godfred Dodzie Amuzu is married to Mrs. Angela Amuzu and is blessed with three children: Joshua, Joseph, and Esther.